THE  TIMES

HOW TO
CRACK
CRYPTIC
CROSSWORDS

TIM MOOREY

Includes 15 practice puzzles from the *Daily Mail*,
The Times, *The Sunday Times*, the *Daily Telegraph*,
the *Sunday Telegraph*, the *Financial Times*, the *Guardian*,
the *Independent*, the *Independent on Sunday*,
the *i Newspaper*, the *Observer*, the *Oldie*, *The Week*,
MoneyWeek, the *Oxford Times*

TIMES
BOOKS

HarperCollins Publishers
Westerhill Road
Bishopbriggs
Glasgow
G64 2QT

www.harpercollins.co.uk

Collins is a registered trademark of HarperCollinsPublishers Ltd

First published in 2014

Copyright © Tim Moorey 2014

Puzzles © *Daily Mail*, *Daily Telegraph*, *Sunday Telegraph* 2014

5

A catalogue record for this book is available from the British Library

ISBN 978-0-00-754652-7

Printed and bound in Great Britain by Clays Ltd, St Ives plc.

Design and layout by Susie Bell – www.f-12.co.uk

MIX
Paper from
responsible sources
FSC™ C007454
www.fsc.org

FSC™ is a non-profit international organisation established to promote
the responsible management of the world's forests. Products carrying the
FSC label are independently certified to assure consumers that they come
from forests that are managed to meet the social, economic and
ecological needs of present and future generations,
and other controlled sources.

Find out more about HarperCollins and the environment at
www.harpercollins.co.uk/green

Contents

To my musician friends in the London Symphony Orchestra, some of whom are managing to crack cryptics after reading my previous book, and all of whom have consistently given me immense musical pleasure over many years.

Foreword

After many years of struggling to make sense of the cryptic clues contained in the crosswords published in the daily papers such as *The Times*, *Telegraph* and *Observer*, I commenced on my retirement in 2002 to tackle the crossword that regularly appeared in *The Week* magazine which was delivered every Friday. Over the next few years I found that I could answer some of the clues as I got to understand and decode the language used by the setter, Tim Moorey.

At this stage in 2008, I started to seek out relevant books and courses that might help me and then discovered that Tim Moorey held weekend workshops on demystifying cryptic crosswords. On checking out his website I found that he was about to provide a Sunday afternoon talk about cryptic crosswords at the Farncombe adult education centre near Evesham. Both I and my wife attended Tim's enjoyable entertaining but thought-provoking presentation about cryptic clues based on the extensive vocabulary of the English language and about the various setters for the national newspapers. Afterwards I purchased a copy of the recently published book *How to Master The Times Crossword*. I only had to flick through a few pages to know that I had, at last, found the book that clearly explained the thought processes that lie behind the cryptic language used by the crossword setters.

Once home I started to work through Tim's book and found I could follow his clear definitions, examples and solutions for the differing types of cryptic clue. With the tutorial style for working through a number of puzzles methodically I felt that I was beginning to get into the crossword clue setter's mind.

Having whetted my appetite with Tim's book I and my wife quickly enrolled onto one of Tim's weekend workshops in early 2009 and we both experienced the sheer delight in cracking the codes of selected cryptic crosswords from a range of the national newspapers in a cooperative, not competitive environment. The course clearly explained in an informal presentation all of the cryptic clue types, all of the abbreviations used by all setters, and, best of all, how to actually tackle the crossword and break the ice to answer the first clue.

The workshop essentially is the practical application of the contents of Tim's book. If you cannot afford the time to attend one of Tim's workshops then you must buy this book. It really reveals everything you need to know about the wonderful pastime of deciphering the code of the clues for cryptic crossword solving. I now have the satisfaction of regularly completing the crossword each week in *The Week* but I now regularly tackle and occasionally succeed with other setter's crosswords in *The Times*, *Telegraph*, *Observer* and *The Oldie*. My enjoyment of this range of puzzles is all due to the application of the rules, examples and methods that are distributed throughout the 200-plus pages of this small masterpiece. If you want, like me, to enjoy the thrill and satisfaction of completing a cryptic crossword then this updated book now covering a range of daily, weekly and monthly publications is the book to diligently work through. You will enjoy many hours of mental exercise and sheer enjoyment at deciphering the clever clue structure that is now an established British pastime.

Happy reading with a sharp rubber-ended pencil to hand.

Tony Savage
A crossword solver

Introduction

In Victorian times a popular game was Magic Square... In 1913 Arthur Wynne was given the task of devising a new puzzle for the World. He adapted the magic square by blackening in some squares and criss-crossing the words. Thus was the first ever crossword puzzle created.

The Advertiser, Adelaide

What's the aim of this book?

I hope to show that, for any daily or weekly crossword puzzle, it is possible substantially to improve your solving skills by the study and application of a few straightforward rules and techniques.

So, is this book only for beginners?

Not at all, it is also for anyone wanting to master crossword puzzles so he or she isn't regularly left with unfinished clues before the next day's newspaper arrives. It may also appeal to others happy to enjoy many first-rate clues and practice puzzles from the sources that abound in the book.

Is there a typical person who might benefit?

Whilst I wouldn't wish to deter others, the person who enjoys a daily struggle with a Quick (non-cryptic) crossword appearing in nearly every newspaper, is an ideal recruit to the world of cryptics. He or she will soon find that they are being given only one way of cracking a clue ie by definition only; cryptics more often than not have two ways, sometimes more, and take full advantage of the delights and richness of the English language.

What are my qualifications?

I offer four:
1. A (not very fast) solver of crosswords for over 50 years, starting with the *London Evening News*, followed by the *Radio Times* and the *News Chronicle*.
2. A crossword setter whose first quick crossword was published in the *Evening News* in 1956, and now for the *Sunday Times*,

Sunday Telegraph, *The Week* and *MoneyWeek* magazines, and other national media for over 25 years.

3. A tutor of 'demystification' fun workshops, mainly for adults but also increasingly for children in schools, held in the UK for over 15 years.

4. Author of *How to Master The Times Crossword* (HarperCollins 2008) which explained cryptic clues in innovatory charts that have been well-received and are used in this book.

Is this then an update of *How to Master The Times Crossword*?

Much feedback on this first book showed that it proved useful for solving crosswords other than The Times'. This encouraged me to write a generic book applicable to just about any crossword. Whilst the teaching parts in Chapters 1 and 2 are pretty much unchanged, all the practice clues and puzzles in Part 3 are new and from a wide variety of sources. These may even offer a reason for previous readers to enjoy this second book.

Are there rules and principles for all cryptic crosswords?

It surprises people to hear that there are, as set down by Ximenes (see box) and they are followed to a large extent by the clue-writers and crossword setters whose work appears here.

So which crosswords are not covered?

Barred crosswords such Mephisto (Sunday Times), Azed (Observer) and the Listener Crossword (in The Times on Saturday) are not used as examples. That's not to say they do not follow Ximenean rules as they indeed do, but solvers of these puzzles at the top of the difficulty scale are unlikely to be in need of instruction.

Also one or two setters in national papers are encouraged to think outside the Ximenean box, arguably good for the development of crosswords but impossible for any tutor to teach.

More of this later.

What about Jumbo crosswords?

No examples of these puzzles are included on the grounds of space but the clueing and solving principles and practice described are just as relevant to their solvers.

What's the book's focus?

It's firmly on the solver. The teaching sections have been written after consulting a large number of solver friends, colleagues, acquaintances and workshop students, much of whose experience and techniques are incorporated. To this end, a setter's blog in the previous book is replaced by practice puzzles.

Are there rules for solving?

No, and I certainly would not wish to be seen as laying rules down. Everyone finds their own way of doing crosswords and my hope is that I help you to find yours. Also I invite you to adopt or reject the tips according to whether they suit you.

One thing I will point out, albeit hesitantly, is that on my workshops, female students tend to be 'instinctive' solvers (initial guess and work out why afterwards) whereas male students tend to be more 'analytical' in their initial solving. But that's naturally not always the case: the key point is that it doesn't matter which type you are.

XIMENES AND AZED

Having taken his name from a Grand Inquisitor in the Spanish Inquisition, Ximenes (Derrick Macnutt), a Marlborough College student and Classics master at Christ's Hospital, was long-term setter of a crossword puzzle in the *Observer*. He is remembered today, not just for his puzzles, but also because he set out fair and consistent principles for cryptic crosswords, design and clues in a ground-breaking 1966 book *Ximenes on the Art of the Crossword*, reissued in 2001. His successor Azed and the majority of setters today in national media follow virtually all of what are known as 'Ximenean' principles.

How to reinforce the teaching?

I follow the well-established teaching principle that adults learn best by doing, rather than reading or being talked at. So I have included lots of practice clues and puzzles, with detailed notes. Slightly slimmed down, these notes are, I hope even clearer to follow than before, setting out the solutions to every practice clue and puzzle. They should leave you in no doubt about why the solutions are what they are, a common frustration for solvers. Finally, a full index is designed to encourage the book's continual use as a manual, rather than a book that you read once and then donate to Oxfam.

The practice clues in Chapter 3 come from varied sources too and many are to savour, as they originally appeared after having been selected as the 'The Clue of The Week', a feature of *The Week* magazine almost since its inception 15 years ago.

Why do people shy away from cryptics?

There are many fears and misapprehensions about the cryptic crossword, usually displayed at the start of my workshops. It is commonly thought that:

- you require a good knowledge of rare words, literature and the classics
- answers are ambiguous
- the cryptic is always harder than the Quick, non-cryptic puzzle
- there are no rules
- you need to have 'that sort of mind'

I hope by the end of this book to have dispelled, partly or wholly, all of these myths.

What sort of knowledge is needed?

I believe that any moderately well-educated person with a love of language and problem-solving, and average general knowledge can complete a cryptic crossword. On these points, Richard Browne, the recently retired *Times* crossword editor, has explained:

'Twenty years ago setters could confidently expect that most solvers would have a reasonable acquaintance with the principal plays of Shakespeare, the main characters and events in the Bible, probably a bit of Milton, a few lyric verses, Dickens perhaps, certainly Sherlock Holmes and some staples of the Victorian nursery such as Lear and Lewis Carroll, and you could confidently clue a word just with a reference. That doesn't work any more, partly because the world has widened up so much.

We have lots of people in this country now from different backgrounds – India, Africa, America, whatever – who have a different system of education, and of course we have people logging on worldwide to *Times* Online, doing the crossword. So it's a larger and more varied audience – you're no longer talking exclusively to the public-school, Oxbridge types who were the core of your readership 50 or 60 years ago.'

Importantly, these comments apply to most cryptics published today.

Finally, why do crosswords?

'I always do the crossword first thing in the morning, to see if I've enough marbles left to make it worth my while getting up.'

Letter to *The Times* from an elderly reader

There is indeed scientific evidence that tackling a crossword can be good for you. Medical research continues to support the notion that mental exercise from activities such as crosswords is beneficial, especially in later life, and stimulates the brain. A New York neurologist, Doctor Joe Verghese, conducted research in this area for over 21 years and found that those who kept their minds nimble were 75 per cent less likely to develop dementia or Alzheimer's disease.

'Do something that is mentally challenging to you,' he has said. 'It seems that remaining mentally agile makes the brain more healthy and more likely to resist illness, just as physical exercise can protect the body from disease.'

In addition, are crosswords educational? I say yes, in the sense that they can improve your vocabulary and general knowledge.

Incidentally, you can check the number of words in your vocabulary via, amongst other sites, www.testyourvocab.com, against the average native English speaker's 27,000 words. Maybe one plan is for you to check your score again after you have mastered this book!

It's now time to get stuck into some basics, in which I assume no previous knowledge whatever.

PART 1

CROSSWORD BASICS

1: Terminology

> 'She had another look at The Times Crossword. The clues might as
> well have been written in a foreign language.'
> Simon Brett, *The Stabbing in the Stables*

The first three chapters establish the terms used throughout. They
are essential reading for beginners, and perhaps also for some seasoned solvers who may have become used to different terminology.

What is a cryptic clue?

A cryptic clue is a sentence or phrase, involving a degree of deception, making sense and frequently conjuring an image, or triggering
thoughts, in its surface reading, but when read in another way can
be decoded using a limited number of well-established techniques
to give a solution. Thus 'cryptic' is used in its meaning of hidden or
misleading.

These are the other terms we shall use:

- Answers to **clues**, running across and down are entered into a
  grid, popularly a diagram, which has **across** and **down** empty
  squares to be filled.
- The grids in the case of the puzzles we are considering here
  contain black square **blocks**, hence they are seen in **blocked**
  puzzles.
- The other main type not being considered here has a grid
  with **bars** rather than blocks, hence the term **barred** puzzles.
- Clue answers are variously called **solutions**, **entries** and
  indeed **answers**.
- Where a solution letter, or letters, is able to be confirmed by
  intersecting entries, they are **checked** letters. **Unchecked**
  letters (**unches** in the trade) are therefore the opposite: the
  solver has no second way of confirming them.

- The person responsible for the crossword is a **setter**; more commonly, but in a term less attractive to most crossword professionals, a **compiler**.
- The term **constructor**, which suits puzzles with difficult-to-build grids, is used in North America.
- Other terms associated with clues such as **wordplay**, **anagram, indicator** and **anagram fodder** are explained as we meet them.

For completeness, there is a rarely used crossword term – **light** – whose meaning has fluctuated somewhat from the early days of crosswords but is defined by the *Collins English Dictionary* today as the solution to a clue.

ARE CRYPTICS EXCLUSIVELY BRITISH?

Commonwealth countries such as Canada, Australia, New Zealand, India, Kenya, Malta and South Africa have daily cryptics similar to British ones, as does Ireland. US crosswords are different in that grids are more open and clues are mildly cryptic or straightforward definitions. There are some occasional British-style puzzles in the *New York Times* and elsewhere. Nonetheless the UK can be considered the home of cryptics. For example, *Daily Telegraph* crosswords are syndicated to around 20 countries.

2: Overview of Clues and Indicators

> 'The question is,' said Alice, 'whether you can make words mean so many different things.'
>
> Lewis Carroll, *Through the Looking Glass*

In this chapter I provide a short overview of the basics of clues and how to recognize them. Detailed points on each clue type are the subject of Chapter 3.

Characteristics of a cryptic clue

We will consider twelve types of cryptic clue, of which the majority conform to the principles contained in this image:

Cryptic clues (mostly) have two parts

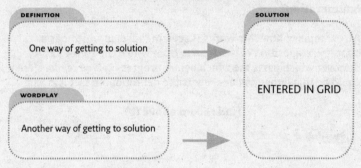

Either the definition or the wordplay can come first in the clue sentence; and either could be exploited first to obtain the solution. Whichever does come second in your solving order acts as confirmation that you have the correct solution.

Taking each element in turn:

Definition: The definition can
- take the form of a word, or words in a phrase
- be an example of the solution (e.g. *fruit* can be defined as *apple, perhaps*)

- be a (misleadingly expressed) synonym of the solution. To this end, definitions are often words that have more than one meaning

Wordplay: This is the way to elicit the solution if the definition does not do so. It can be seen as either:

- the letters of the solution needing manipulation in one of several ways to provide another indication of the definition, *or*
- individual word or words in the clue having to be interpreted in a different way from the surface meaning

Perhaps strictly accurately the terms should be **word** and **letterplay** (though not, as an elderly student once stumbled over, 'loveplay'!).

> **TOP TIP – DEFINITION PLACEMENT**
> Beginners find it much easier to decode a cryptic clue when they are told that the **definition** is almost always either at the beginning or end of the clue sentence or phrase.

Solution: This can be one or more words whose word-length is shown at the end of the clue in parentheses (sometimes called the **enumeration**).

An example of how this works is seen in this clue which has a simple juxtaposition of three parts from which the solver has to discover which parts are which before progress can be made. Here it could be that either *find* or *above* is the definition. In fact it is *find*.

Find record above (8)

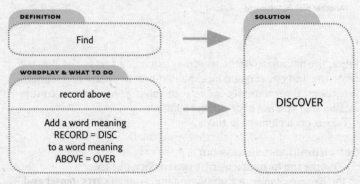

Linkwords: Few clues are as straightforward in construction as the previous example and the first mild challenge is that there is often a linkword between the two parts to give the solution. The chart then is:

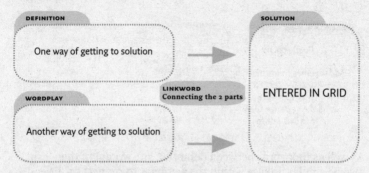

CRYPTIC CLUES WITH LINKING WORDS

Below is a clue which also starts with the definition but, in addition, has a linkword, one that is commonly used: *from*. The sense conveyed by *from* is that a synonym for church house can be formed from the two parts *earlier* and *years* (if the latter is taken as an abbreviation – more on this later).

Church house from earlier years (6)

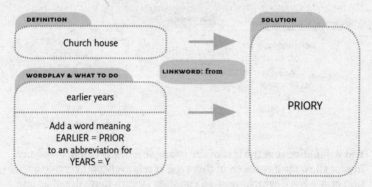

Next is an example in which the definition is the final word in the clue and in which the linkword is *in*, the sense being that the wordplay is *seen in* the solution. This is a trickier clue than we have seen so far, as the solution *tea service* is split into two parts, *teaser* and *vice*, to form the wordplay.

Puzzle failing in China (3, 7)

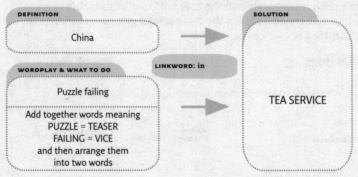

As well as linkwords between definition and wordplay, there can also be similar linkage within the wordplay to connect its different parts. Here it is *and*, a simple additive indication. The other linkword *is* indicates that the definition can be formed from the wordplay.

ADDITIVE CLUE: What babies need is sleep and food (7)

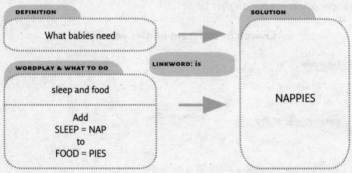

You will notice that the last of the example clues is labelled *additive*. In fact all so far have been of this type, a relatively plain construction of A + B = C which we shall consider later in more detail as one of the twelve clue types, dividing these into one group of eight and one group of four. Why split clues into two groups? Because some always contain the means of identifying their type (the **first eight**) and others virtually always do not (the **remaining four**). This distinction is amplified in the section which follows.

Indicators

At this point, beginners tend to say:

'Yes, I know that there are different types of clue but how on earth do I know which is which?'

The answer is as follows. For the **first group of eight** there is always a signpost to the solution, called the indicator, within the clue sentence. Remember, an indicator is the means of identifying clue types. In Chapter 3 we will consider the specific indicators for the first group of eight clue types. In the example the indicator is *wrong*, showing that this is an **anagram** clue. The concept behind this indicator is that the letters to be mixed are incorrect and must be changed to form the solution. There are many ways of giving the same anagram instruction to solvers, as you will also see in Chapter 3.

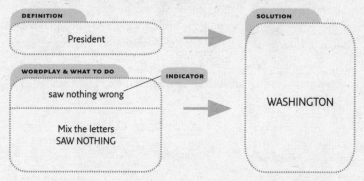

ANAGRAM CLUE: President saw nothing wrong (10)

DEFINITION

President

WORDPLAY & WHAT TO DO · INDICATOR

saw nothing wrong

Mix the letters
SAW NOTHING

SOLUTION

WASHINGTON

For the **remaining group of four**, it's usually a case of informed guesswork rather than indicators. This may seem unreasonable and impossible for the novice solver but I aim to prove that this is not really the case.

In the meantime, this may be a good time to point out that trial and error and/or inspired guesswork are part and parcel of good solving. This is reinforced by the clueing practice of all good setters whereby the clue type will nearly always become clear on working backwards from the solutions. Indeed, when a solver sees the solution the following day, he or she should only rarely be left thinking (as Ximenes put it):

'I thought of that but I couldn't see how it could be right.'

We will now proceed to examine in detail all clue types and their indicators, with one and sometimes two examples of each type.

3: Clue Types and Indicators in Detail

'Give us a kind of clue.' W.S. Gilbert, *Utopia Limited*

Until Chapter 8, we'll keep it simple with regard to clue types.
In later chapters we will see that the clue types can and often do
overlap, involving more than one sort of manipulation of letters or
words within any one clue.

The first eight clue types

We will now examine each of the eight clue types in detail, together
with their indicators, and offer some example clues. To give yourself
solving practice, you may wish from now on to cover up the bottom
half of the diagram that contains the solution and wordplay.

The first eight types are shown in the circular chart below, and we
shall take each in turn, working clockwise from the top.

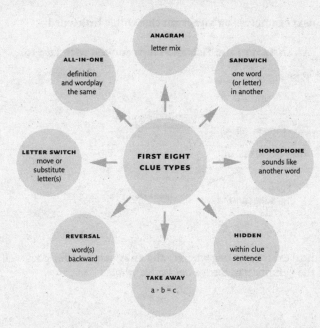

1. The anagram clue

An anagram, sometimes termed a **letter mix**, is a rearrangement of letters or words within the clue sentence to form the solution word or words.

The letters to be mixed (the **anagram fodder**) may or may not include an abbreviation, a routine trick for old hands but, as I have observed, a cause of some discomfort for first-timers.

ANAGRAM CLUE: Mum, listen for a change (6)

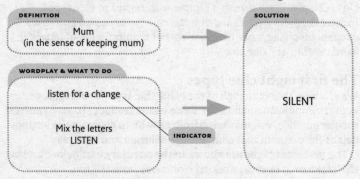

This next example is an **anagram** clue with a **linkword**:

ANAGRAM CLUE: Fish and chips cooked with lard (9)

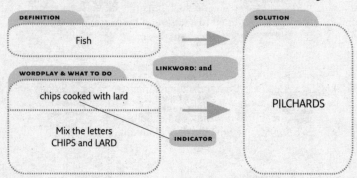

The third example is one wherein the **anagram fodder** goes well with the definition to form a believable whole:

ANAGRAM CLUE: The new stadium designed for a football club (4,3,6)

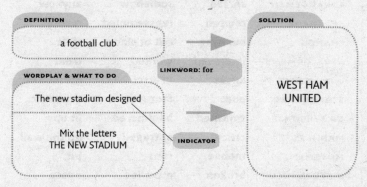

DEFINITION

a football club

SOLUTION

WEST HAM UNITED

WORDPLAY & WHAT TO DO

LINKWORD: for

The new stadium designed

Mix the letters
THE NEW STADIUM

INDICATOR

For is a linkword here in the sense that the wordplay is to be arranged *for* the answer. The essential point for indicators of **anagram** clues is that they show a rearrangement, a disturbance to the natural order or a change to be made. There are very many ways of doing this, some reasonably straightforward but others requiring a stretch of the imagination. For example, words and phrases related to drunkenness and madness have to be taken as involving disturbance so that *stoned*, *pickled*, *tight*, *bananas*, *nuts*, *crackers* and *out to lunch* could all be misleading ways to indicate an anagram. I am often asked for a comprehensive list but, because there are so many, unfortunately there is no such list. The table that follows on the next page is designed to expand on the various categories of rearrangement by giving a few examples of each overleaf:

> **TOP TIP - ANAGRAMS**
> Early crosswords did not indicate an anagram; solvers were required to guess that a mixture of letters was needed. This is universally regarded as unfair on the solver so that there will always nowadays be an indication of an anagram.

INDICATORS FOR ANAGRAM CLUES

ARRANGEMENT	sorted	somehow	anyhow
REARRANGEMENT	revised	reassembled	resort
CHANGE	bursting	out of place	shift
DEVELOPMENT	improved	worked	treat
WRONGNESS	amiss	in error	messed up
STRANGENESS	odd	fantastic	eccentric
DRUNKENNESS	smashed	hammered	lit up
MADNESS	crazy	outraged	up the wall
MOVEMENT	mobile	runs	hit
DISTURBANCE OF ORDER	broken	muddled	upset
INVOLVEMENT	complicated	tangled	implicated

2. The sandwich clue

A sandwich can be considered as bread outside some filling. Similarly in this clue type, the solution can be built from one part being either put **outside** another part or being put **inside** another part.

This is an example of **outside** (with an abbreviation to be made in wordplay):

SANDWICH CLUE: Simple mug holding one litre (6)

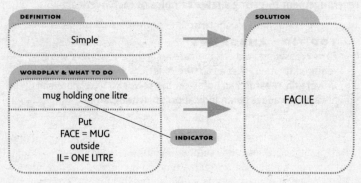

DEFINITION	SOLUTION
Simple	

WORDPLAY & WHAT TO DO	
mug holding one litre	FACILE
Put FACE = MUG outside IL = ONE LITRE	INDICATOR

This is an example of **inside** with a clear instruction as to what's to be done:

SANDWICH CLUE: **Family member put us in the money (6)**

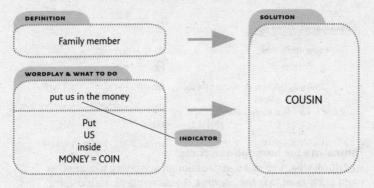

DEFINITION	
Family member	→

WORDPLAY & WHAT TO DO	
put us in the money	→
Put US inside MONEY = COIN	INDICATOR

SOLUTION
COUSIN

Note that *about* has multiple uses in crosswords (see Chapter 10).

SOME INDICATORS FOR SANDWICH CLUES

OUTSIDE	contains	clothing	boxing
	houses	harbours	carries
	grasping	enclosing	including
	restrains	protecting	about
INSIDE	breaks	cuts	boring
	piercing	penetrating	fills
	enters	interrupting	amidst
	held by	occupies	splitting

3. The homophone clue

In this type, the solution sounds like another word given by the wordplay. The clue is often fairly easy to recognize but it may be harder to find the two words which sound alike.

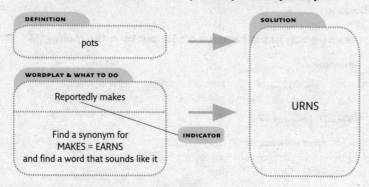

HOMOPHONE CLUE: Reportedly makes pots (4)

DEFINITION

pots

SOLUTION

WORDPLAY & WHAT TO DO

Reportedly makes

Find a synonym for
MAKES = EARNS
and find a word that sounds like it

INDICATOR

URNS

Indicators for homophone clues:

Anything which gives an impression of sounding like another word such as *so to speak*, *we hear*, *it's said* acts as an indicator. This extends to what's heard in different real-life situations; for example, at home it could be *on the radio*; in the theatre it could be *to an audience*; in the office it could be *for an auditor*.

4. The hidden clue

A hidden clue is arguably the easiest type to solve. That's because the letters to be uncovered require no change: they just need to be dug out of the sentence designed to conceal them. In the first example, the indicator is *in*:

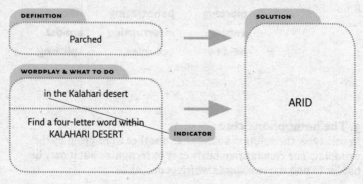

HIDDEN CLUE: Parched in the Kalahari desert (4)

DEFINITION

Parched

SOLUTION

WORDPLAY & WHAT TO DO

in the Kalahari desert

Find a four-letter word within
KALAHARI DESERT

INDICATOR

ARID

Indicators for hidden clues:
Commonly *some* (in the sense of a certain part of what follows), *some of*, *partly*, are unique to **hidden** clues; *within*, *amidst*, *holding* and *in* can be either **hidden** or **sandwich** indicators.

A variant of the **hidden** clue is where the letters are concealed at intervals within the wordplay, most commonly odd or even letters. You are asked to extract letters that appear as, say, the first, third and fifth letters in the wordplay section of the clue sentence and ignore the intervening letters. Note that there would not normally be superfluous words in such a clue sentence, making it easier to be certain which letters are involved in the extraction.

Here is one such clue in which you have to take only the odd letters of *culture* for the solution.

HIDDEN CLUE: Odd bits of culture such as this (4)

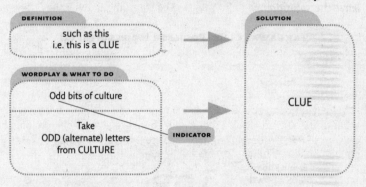

Some indicators for hidden-at-intervals clues:
Oddly, evenly, regularly, ignoring the odds, alternately.

5. The takeaway clue
A **takeaway** clue involves something being deducted from something else. This can be one or more letters or a whole word. In the example below it's one letter, *R*, which is an abbreviation of *right*, and *get* is an instruction to the solver. It should be noted that sometimes you will find abbreviations signposted, e.g. 'a small street', more usually not, e.g. 'street'. You will find in the Appendices a list of those most frequently appearing in crosswords and all of those used in the clues and puzzles of this book.

TAKEAWAY CLUE: Get employed right away in Surrey town (6)

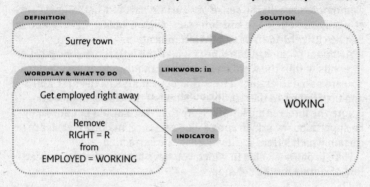

In our second example, it's the first letter that is to be taken away to leave the solution:

TAKEAWAY CLUE: Possess a topless dress (3)

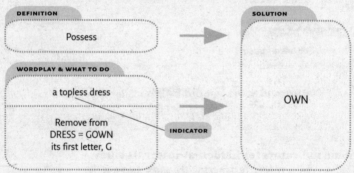

Indicators for takeaway clues:

These tend to be self-explanatory, such as *reduced*, *less*, *extracted*, but, beware, they can be highly misleading, such as *cast* in a clue concerning the theatre, or *shed* in one ostensibly about the garden. Some indicators inform us that a single letter is to be taken away. These include *short*, *almost*, *briefly*, *nearly* and *most of*, all signifying by long-established convention that the final letter of a word is to be removed. There is more on **takeaway** indicators such as *unopened*, *disheartened*, *needing no introduction* and *endless* on pages 31–33, which deal with **letter selection** indicators.

6. The reversal clue

The whole of a solution can sometimes be reversed to form another entirely different word. In addition, writing letters backwards or upwards is often part of a clue's wordplay, but for the time being we are concerned with reversal providing the whole of the answer. This is a clue for an across solution:

REVERSAL CLUE: Knock back beer like a king (5)

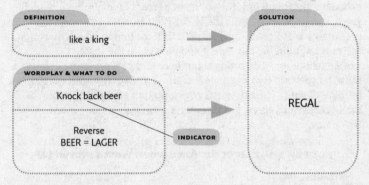

This is a reversal clue for a down solution (see below for an explanation of why this matters):

REVERSAL CLUE: Put out by mounting objections (4)

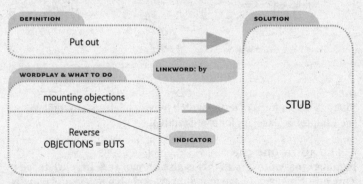

Indicators for reversal clues:

Anything showing backward movement, e.g. *around*, *over*, *back*, *recalled*.

Do be aware that some **reversal** indicators apply to **down** clues only, reflecting their position in the grid. The example above of a **down** clue uses *mounting* for this purpose; other possibilities are *overturned*, *raised*, *up*, *on the way up* and *served up*.

7. The letter switch clue

Where two words differ from each other by one or more letters, this can be exploited by setters so that moving one or more letters produces another word, the solution. Here is an example in which you are instructed to shift the *W* for *West* in *when* in a way that produces a word meaning *axed*. You are not told in which direction the move should be, but here it can only be to the right.

An extra point to be brought out here is that if a pause or comma after the first two words is imagined, the instruction should become clearer. This imaginary punctuation effect is common to many crossword clues; see Chapter 4, pages 40–42, for more on this point.

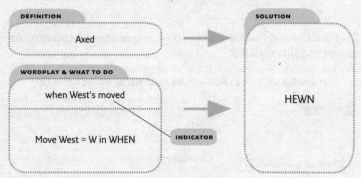

LETTER SWITCH CLUE: Axed when West's moved (4)

DEFINITION

Axed

WORDPLAY & WHAT TO DO

when West's moved

Move West = W in WHEN   INDICATOR

SOLUTION

HEWN

There is also a form of letter switch in which letters are replaced; see Chapter 8, page 70, for more on this.

8. The all-in-one clue

In many crossword circles this is also known as **& lit**, christened by Ximenes. However, I have found my workshop participants usually consider this too cryptic a name! It actually means 'and is literally so' but people tend to puzzle over that at the expense of understanding the concept.

In fact, it is a simple one that I prefer to call **all-in-one**, which is what it is: the definition and wordplay are combined into one, often shortish sentence which, when decoded, leads to a description of the solution.

ALL-IN-ONE CLUE: Heads of the several amalgamated Russian states (5)

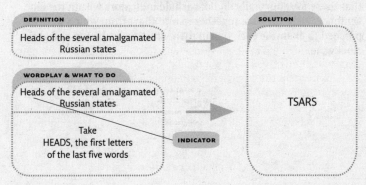

This clue relies on the **letter selection** indicator *heads* (see page 31) to provide the solution. Most of the clueing techniques outlined earlier can be used to make an **all-in-one** clue (see examples in Chapter 8), always providing that the definition and wordplay are one and the same.

Probably the commonest type is an **all-in-one anagram**, with an anagram as part or all of the wordplay and no extra definition needed because it has been provided by the wordplay. Here is an example:

ALL-IN-ONE ANAGRAM CLUE: A pot's stirred with one? (8)

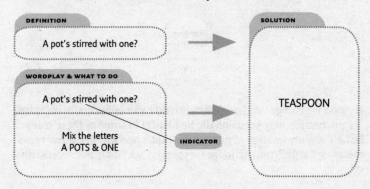

Incidentally, this clue demonstrates how punctuation can give you some help with a clue. The question mark is telling you that a pot isn't necessarily stirred with a spoon but it may be. For examples of when punctuation is not so helpful, see Chapter 4 (page 40–41).

The remaining four types

Now we will focus on the remaining four clue types. Remember that these four normally do not include indicators within the clue sentence. Here they are together in one chart from which we will proceed to examine each one in turn, starting at the top and going clockwise.

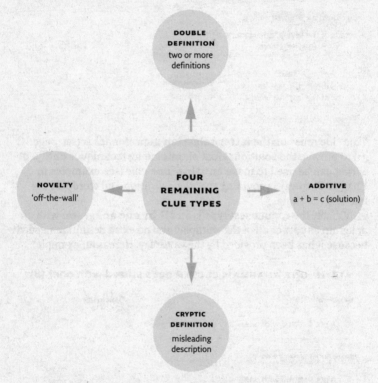

How do we recognize these when no indicator is normally included?

Punctuation may occasionally be helpful in some of these clues but it's mainly intelligent guesswork that's needed. Are these types therefore harder? You can judge for yourself but I'd say not necessarily.

9. The double definition clue

This is simply two, or very occasionally more, definitions of the solution side by side. There may be a linking word, as in the second example, such as *is* or *'s*, but most frequently there is none, as in this clue.

DOUBLE DEFINITION CLUE 1: Shoots game (5)

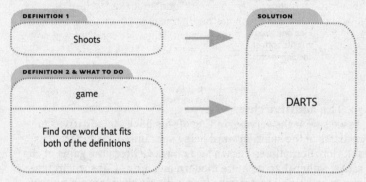

DEFINITION 1

Shoots

DEFINITION 2 & WHAT TO DO

game

Find one word that fits both of the definitions

SOLUTION

DARTS

DOUBLE DEFINITION CLUE 2: Pools entries making one a rich man (5)

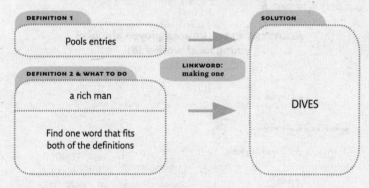

DEFINITION 1

Pools entries

LINKWORD: making one

DEFINITION 2 & WHAT TO DO

a rich man

Find one word that fits both of the definitions

SOLUTION

DIVES

Indicators for double definition clues:

To repeat, no specific indicator is ever given. It can nonetheless often be guessed by its shortness, or by two or more words, lacking an obvious linkword. With only two or three words in a clue, there's a good chance it's a **double definition**. One way of spotting this type of clue is an *and* in a short clue, e.g. *Bit of butter and jam (6)* for *scrape*:

DOUBLE DEFINITION CLUE 3: Bit of butter and jam (6)

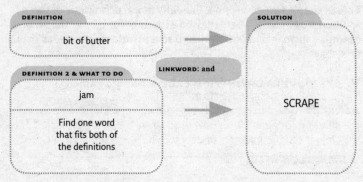

DEFINITION

bit of butter

LINKWORD: and

DEFINITION 2 & WHAT TO DO

jam

Find one word
that fits both of
the definitions

SOLUTION

SCRAPE

10. The additive clue

As we saw at the very beginning of this book, an **additive** clue consists of the solution word being split into parts to form the solution. Sometimes known as a **charade** (from the game of charades, rather than its more modern meaning of 'absurd pretence'), it may be helpful to describe it as a simple algebraic expression A + B = solution C. Here is one with several misleading aspects. Note the use of the linking phrase *employed ahead of*, telling you to join part A to part B:

ADDITIVE CLUE: Pole employed ahead of young local worker (8)

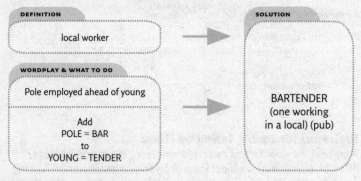

DEFINITION

local worker

WORDPLAY & WHAT TO DO

Pole employed ahead of young

Add
POLE = BAR
to
YOUNG = TENDER

SOLUTION

BARTENDER
(one working
in a local) (pub)

Indicators for additive clues:

With no specific indicator, it's a question rather of spotting that A + B can give C, the solution. Sometimes this is made easier by linkwords such as *employed ahead of* (as in the earlier clue), *facing*, *alongside*, *with*, *next to*, indicating that the parts A and B have to be set alongside each other. In the case of **down** clues, the corresponding linkwords would be *on top of*, *looking down on* and similar expressions reflecting the grid position of letters to be entered.

11. The cryptic definition clue

There are no component parts at all to this clue, which consists simply of a misleading, usually one-dimensional, way to describe the solution. Depending on how much information is imparted by the clue, it can be very easy or very tough. The best of these clues have an amusing or whimsical air, as in both these examples:

CRYPTIC DEFINITION CLUE 1:
Women can't stand going there (6)

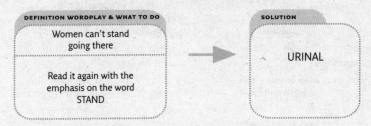

DEFINITION WORDPLAY & WHAT TO DO	SOLUTION
Women can't stand going there	URINAL
Read it again with the emphasis on the word STAND	

CRYPTIC DEFINITION CLUE 1: He's been known to pot the white (8)

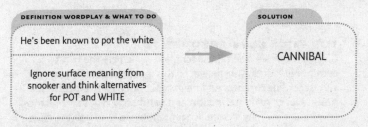

DEFINITION WORDPLAY & WHAT TO DO	SOLUTION
He's been known to pot the white	CANNIBAL
Ignore surface meaning from snooker and think alternatives for POT and WHITE	

Indicators for cryptic definitions:

The nature of this clue type is such that no indicator is ever given. It can be identified either from the fact that nothing in the clue looks like an indicator, and/or from the presence of a question mark. A tip is to look hard at words which have more than one meaning and then think below the surface. Otherwise, wait until some intersecting letters are available.

12. The novelty clue

From the inception of crypticity in crosswords, there have been innovative clues conforming to no single pattern which defy categorization into any of the preceding groups. These clues are often solved with extra pleasure.

The setter has found it possible to exploit coincidences or special features of a word. As with the cryptic definition type, the solver is asked to think laterally and throw away any misleading images created by the clue. In some rare circumstances when an especially novel idea is used, there may not even be a proper definition. There are more examples of the **novelty** clue in Chapter 8 but, as a taster, here is one:

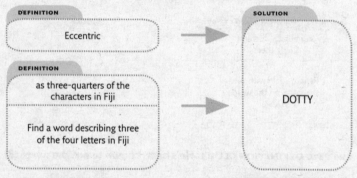

NOVELTY CLUE:
Eccentric as three-quarters of the characters in Fiji? (5)

DEFINITION
Eccentric

DEFINITION
as three-quarters of the characters in Fiji

Find a word describing three of the four letters in Fiji

SOLUTION
DOTTY

TOP TIP – CLUE FREQUENCY
Given the twelve clue types identified, which are the most commonly found? The answer to this is that frequency patterns vary according to setter and newspaper but that the **additive**, **anagram**, **cryptic definition** and **sandwich** types are the most common; they may indeed account for more than half the clues in many crosswords. It may help you to know that there are rarely more than two or three of the following types in any one puzzle: **hidden**, **homophone**, **all-in-one**, **novelty**, **letter switch**. As we shall see later, setters make use of more than one type of wordplay within any one clue so that, for example, a **sandwich** clue can include a **reversal**, a **takeaway** or an **anagram** element within it.

Letter selection indicators

Before moving on to solving clues, we have to consider how individual letters within clues are signposted. We have seen what sort of indicators go with what sort of clues; now we'll take a look at another commonly used indicator which is essential to solving skills. Take this clue as an example:

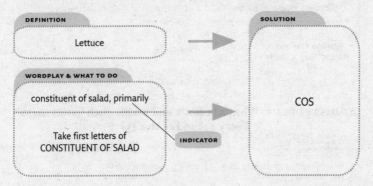

ADDITIVE CLUE: Lettuce constituent of salad, primarily (3)

DEFINITION

Lettuce

SOLUTION

WORDPLAY & WHAT TO DO

constituent of salad, primarily

Take first letters of
CONSTITUENT OF SALAD

INDICATOR

COS

Experienced solvers would be immediately drawn towards the word *primarily* as it indicates that the first letter or (as in this case) letters of the preceding words are to be selected as building blocks to the solution. In more complex clues they could then be subject to further treatment, such as forming part of an anagram, but here they are used simply to form *cos*, the *lettuce* salad ingredient.

There are many alternative ways of showing that the first letter is to be manipulated in some way. Some of these indicators are: *starter, lead, source, opening, top, introduction* and so on. They may be extended to the plural form too with the use of, say, *beginnings, foremost* and *heads*. Note that *bit of, part of* and suchlike always indicate the first letter.

Naturally, other positions within words are indicated in a similar fashion. The last letter can be *end, back, finally, tail* and the middle letter *centre, heart*, and all of the inside letters of a word can be *innards, contents, stuffing*.

In their negative **takeaway** guise, they can be *headless, unopened, failing to start*; and *empty* signifies that the whole of the innards of a word is to be removed.

Overleaf are some examples of letter selection indicators at work:

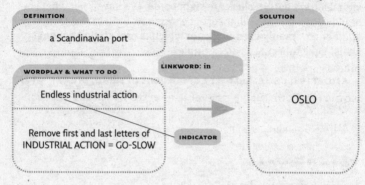

TAKEAWAY CLUE:
Endless industrial action in a Scandinavian port (4)

DEFINITION

a Scandinavian port

SOLUTION

LINKWORD: in

WORDPLAY & WHAT TO DO

Endless industrial action

OSLO

Remove first and last letters of
INDUSTRIAL ACTION = GO-SLOW   INDICATOR

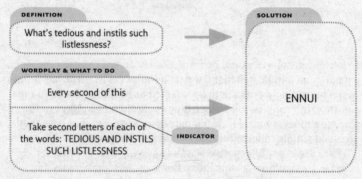

ADDITIVE CLUE: What's tedious and instils such listlessness?
Every second of this (5)

DEFINITION

What's tedious and instils such
listlessness?

SOLUTION

WORDPLAY & WHAT TO DO

Every second of this

ENNUI

Take second letters of each of
the words: TEDIOUS AND INSTILS   INDICATOR
SUCH LISTLESSNESS

After a time, you will become familiar with looking beyond and
through the surface meaning of a word doing duty as an indicator so
that you realize what you are required to do to the relevant letter(s)
or word(s).

Beware **letter selection** indicators that, depending on the setter's
policy, can do double or triple duty:

Endless: takeaway last letter only, or first and last letters.
Head: first letter, or takeaway first letter (in its sense of behead).

Cut: last letter takeaway, sandwich (inside type), anagram (in its slang sense of *drunk*).
Back: last letter, reversal.

Note that in the example below *extremely* indicates first and last letters, in some crosswords it can indicate the last letter only of the preceding word.

ADDITIVE CLUE: Robin's slayer uses extremely sharp weapon (7)

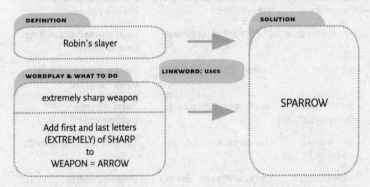

There are examples of indicators throughout this book but it would take an impossibly large volume to include all those used. There are books which list more (as covered in Chapter 13) but even they are not comprehensive. The point to bear in mind is that once you are aware of the possible clue types, you will often be able to infer from a word or words what you are being instructed to do.

What can be difficult, however, is where the same common word in the English language serves as an indicator for several clue types. The words *in* and *about* are the most problematic examples of this and you will find more about these and equally troublesome words in Chapter 10.

Chapters 1–3: summary

Here are two charts offering in summary form the basic points of Chapters 1, 2 and 3. First, a summary of clue types, typical indicators and what the solver must do:

CLUE TYPE	TYPICAL INDICATORS	WHAT TO DO
Types 1–8	Indicators included in clue	
ANAGRAM	New, mixed, changing, drunk, in error	Change letters to another word
SANDWICH (OUTSIDE)	Holding, keeps, contains	Put some letters outside others
SANDWICH (INSIDE)	In, breaks, cutting, interrupts	Put some letters inside others
HOMOPHONE	Mentioned, we hear	Find a word sounding like another
HIDDEN	Some, partly, within	Find a word within other words
REVERSAL (ACROSS CLUE)	Back, over, returns	Turn letters backwards
REVERSAL (DOWN CLUE)	Up, over, served up	Turn letters upwards
TAKEAWAY	Less, without, drop, cast	Deduct some letter(s) from a word
LETTER SWITCH	For, replacing, moving	Exchange or move letters
ALL-IN-ONE	Various, depending on wordplay	Use wordplay to find solution which is then defined by the wordplay
Types 9–12	Indicators (usually) not included in clue	
ADDITIVE	Usually none given	Add letter(s) to other letter(s)
DOUBLE DEFINITION	None given	Find solution from two or more distinct definitions, side by side
CRYPTIC DEFINITION	None given	Find solution from puns, hints, ambiguities; ignore surface reading
NOVELTY	None given	Think laterally

Second, let's see how each clue type (apart from a **novelty** clue) could be applied, using the same solution word in each. That word is *time*, which is defined as *magazine* (the US news magazine) in all but two clues. The indicators are underlined in each clue.

CLUE TYPE	INDICATORS FOR THE WORD 'TIME'	WHAT TO DO
Types 1–8		
ANAGRAM	<u>New</u> item in magazine	Change letters of ITEM
SANDWICH (OUTSIDE)	Match <u>bringing in</u> millions for magazine	Put MATCH = TIE outside MILLIONS = M
SANDWICH (INSIDE)	Millions <u>put into</u> match magazine	Put MILLIONS = M inside MATCH = TIE
HOMOPHONE	Herb <u>mentioned</u> in magazine	Find a word for a HERB sounding like TIME (THYME)
HIDDEN	<u>Some</u> sentimental magazine	Find a word within SENTIMENTAL
REVERSAL (ACROSS CLUE)	Magazine issue <u>backed</u>	Reverse ISSUE = EMIT
REVERSAL (DOWN CLUE)	Magazine issue <u>taken up</u>	Reverse ISSUE = EMIT
TAKEAWAY	<u>Nameless</u> chaps behind note in magazine	Remove NAME = N from MEN and add (musical) NOTE = TI
LETTER SWITCH	Magazine volume, one <u>for</u> nothing	Replace NOTHING = O in VOLUME = TOME with I
ALL-IN-ONE	Male, <u>interned</u> in Windsor is doing this?	Put MALE = M inside WINDSOR = TIE (time served by person interned)
Types 9–12 (except novelty clue)		
ADDITIVE	Note yours truly in magazine	Add NOTE = TI to YOURS TRULY = ME
DOUBLE DEFINITION	Bird magazine	Two ways of expressing time, BIRD is time in prison
CRYPTIC DEFINITION	Wilde did it in a sentence	Think of Oscar W in prison

WHY ARE SOME CLUES MORE DIFFICULT THAN OTHERS?

Levels of cryptic difficulty are shown by these **sandwich** clues, all using the same definition *don't worry* and all giving the same answer but with differing wordplay:

- Ned catches vermin, don't worry (5,4): The letters to be manipulated are in the clue ie *Ned* outside *vermin*
- Edward catches vermin, don't worry (5,4): A small change from *Edward* to *Ned* is required
- Boy catches mice, don't worry (5,4): Two changes are needed as *mice* has to become *vermin*

I hope you got *never mind* as the answer in each case. If you didn't, never mind, as the point remains that while clue structures are the same, synonyms have to be found before the sandwich can be made and it is this that makes solving more difficult. Naturally unusual words as answers and obscure references are other causes of difficulty.

4: Tips for Solving Clues

> 'This isn't biography. It's the only thing the English are good at...
> crossword puzzles.'
> Alan Bennett, *Kafka's Dick*

Having considered clue types and various points associated with each,
we will now consider some tips on how you might go about solving them.

Seasoned solvers have many ways of uncovering a clue's solution.
What follows are some of these from my own toolkit and the others
I have been given for this book. They are in no particular recommended order of importance, except that the first two are often
quoted as ways to get started.

1. Find the definition
As you know by now, the definition part of nearly all clues is either
at the beginning or end of a clue. Identifying it quickly, and assess-
ing the definition in conjunction with word-length shown, allows
the possibility of a good initial guess which can then be checked
against wordplay before entry.

2. Find an indicator and/or clue type
Not all clues have indicators, as we have seen, but where they do,
try to use them to identify the clue type. For example, you may spot
a familiar anagram indicator such as *mixed* or *battered* and thence
compare the letters in the **anagram fodder** with the word-length
of the solution given. If they correspond, there is a good chance
that you have identified the wordplay element of the clue and can
develop that into a possible solution.

3. Ignore the scenario
Setters do their best to produce clues which paint a smooth, realis-
tic picture, often referred to as the *surface meaning* or *surface*. Try to
ignore it however and look at the individual components in front of
you. Take the clue overleaf, seemingly about a party:

ADDITIVE CLUE: Last ones in get no sherry trifle (3)

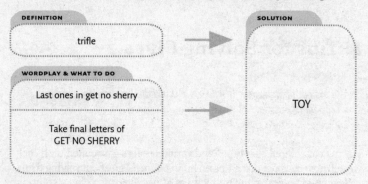

DEFINITION	SOLUTION
trifle	TOY

WORDPLAY & WHAT TO DO

Last ones in get no sherry

Take final letters of
GET NO SHERRY

You can be pretty sure that recalling memories of children's parties will not be productive. It's just a clever deception by the use of *ones* for *letters* and a **letter selection** indicator, *last* (see Chapter 3, page 31), leading to *toy* = *trifle*.

> **TOP TIP – SURFACE MEANING**
> The ability to look beyond surface meaning is what many find the hardest part of cracking a cryptic clue. My advice can only be to keep trying.

4. Exploit word-lengths
Use friendly word-lengths such as 4,2,3,4 with the central two being perhaps something like *in the* or *of the*; and 4,4,1,4 nearly always embracing the letter A, from which something like *once upon a time* may be the guessable answer.

5. Study every word
Consider each word carefully, separately and together. Disregard phrases which go naturally together such as, say, *silver wedding*, and split them into their parts. It could be that the definition is *silver* on its own and *wedding* is part of the wordplay.

In doing this, think of all the meanings of a word rather than the one that comes first into your head.

For example, forget *drink* in its marine sense in the next clue and switch to *alcohol*. The indicator *some* makes it a **hidden clue**.

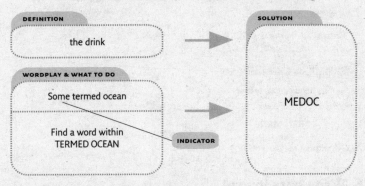

HIDDEN CLUE: Some termed ocean the drink (5)

DEFINITION
the drink

SOLUTION
MEDOC

WORDPLAY & WHAT TO DO
Some termed ocean

Find a word within TERMED OCEAN

INDICATOR

Here is another misleading image in the second example below, which has nothing to do with DIY:

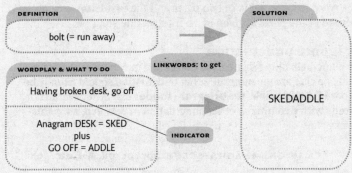

ADDITIVE CLUE INCLUDING ANAGRAM: Having broken desk, go off to get bolt (9)

DEFINITION
bolt (= run away)

SOLUTION
SKEDADDLE

LINKWORDS: to get

WORDPLAY & WHAT TO DO
Having broken desk, go off

Anagram DESK = SKED
plus
GO OFF = ADDLE

INDICATOR

Last, an instance, overleaf, of how separating the sentence into even its smallest parts is sometimes needed. This clue is a further demonstration of a **letter selection** indicator, *empty* for *lane* leaving the two letters *le*, and of a deceptive definition.

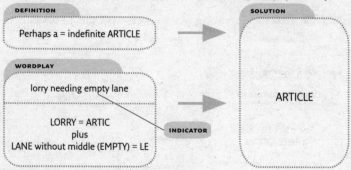

DEFINITION

Perhaps a = indefinite ARTICLE

WORDPLAY

lorry needing empty lane

LORRY = ARTIC
plus
LANE without middle (EMPTY) = LE

INDICATOR

ARTICLE

6. Write bars in grid

Given word-lengths that indicate more than one complete word (e.g. 3-7, or 3,7), some solvers automatically write the word divisions as bar-lines into the grid and find that helps. The bars can be either vertical or horizontal depending on whether they are split words or hyphenated words. This little trick can be especially useful when the word to be found is in two parts and the first letter, say, of the second of the parts is given by an intersecting solution.

7. Ignore punctuation

In a nutshell, only exclamation marks and question marks at the end of a clue are meaningful; other punctuation should usually be ignored. For example, the **anagram fodder** can include letters or words with a comma or other punctuation in between, as in this tricky clue:

ALL-IN-ONE ANAGRAM CLUE: Sort of roll, A-E etc? (9)

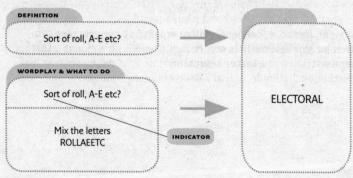

DEFINITION

Sort of roll, A-E etc?

WORDPLAY & WHAT TO DO

Sort of roll, A-E etc?

Mix the letters
ROLLAEETC

INDICATOR

ELECTORAL

Another example of this is seen in the clue that follows:

HIDDEN CLUE: Long wait – check-in's closed (4)

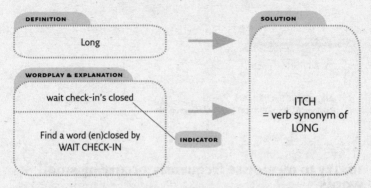

DEFINITION		SOLUTION
Long	→	
WORDPLAY & EXPLANATION		ITCH = verb synonym of LONG
wait check-in's closed		
Find a word (en)closed by WAIT CHECK-IN	INDICATOR	

The dash is to be ignored. There is more on misleading punctuation in Chapter 9, pages 93–96.

8. Think comma

One of the most useful tips I received as a novice was to imagine a comma in any part of the clue sentence. As we have seen in nearly all the examples so far, clues consist frequently of a string of words, each one of which has a part to play, and separating them into their meaningful parts can prove very helpful. In the clue overleaf, imagining a pause between the last two words makes the solution much easier.

9. Guess

An inspired guess can work wonders; you just feel that you know the answer without recognizing why. I have watched this intuitive process in my workshops and it's magical. On one occasion a lady in her late 80s, a solver evidently for almost as long, was often able to come up with the answers before anyone else but had no idea how she had done so. Unfortunately, this method doesn't work for everybody.

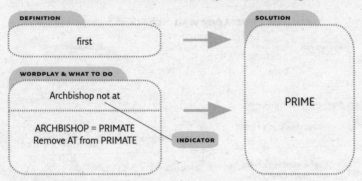

TAKEAWAY CLUE: Archbishop? Not at first (5)

DEFINITION

first

SOLUTION

WORDPLAY & WHAT TO DO

Archbishop not at

PRIME

ARCHBISHOP = PRIMATE
Remove AT from PRIMATE

INDICATOR

10. Try to memorise frequently-occurring small words

The same three- and four-letter words inevitably crop up a lot and successful solvers store up words like *pig*, *sow*, *cow*, *tup* and *hog* for *farm animal* (or even just *animal*) and smartly bring these into their deliberations. I realise that many of my readers will have better things to remember, so let's move on.

11. Advice on cracking anagrams

After you have identified an **anagram** indicator, counted the number of letters in the **anagram fodder**, including any abbreviations, and seen that they make up the given word-length, what techniques are there to find the solution?

People have their own familiar way of sorting out anagrams. Some find using Scrabble cards works well; often the simplest method involves finding the right combination from careful scrutiny of the letters, looking for the commonly occurring *-ing*, *-tion*, *-er*, *-or* endings.

If this does not work, the anagram fodder can then be written down in various ways: in a straight line, in a diamond shape, in a circle, in reverse order or in random order. With longer anagrams, this can involve several rewrites in different orders until the answer emerges. In cases where the definition is something not very specific, such as *plant* or *animal*, it may be best to defer resolution until some intersecting letters have been entered.

Finally there are electronic aids as listed in Chapter 13 which can take all the pain (but maybe some of the enjoyment) out of the process.

5: Tips for Solving the Whole Puzzle

'They say children in kindergarten must play in order to learn. What do they mean, children? Crossword puzzles learned grown folks more words than school teachers.'
Will Rogers

Now let's consider some points for tackling the whole of a puzzle.

1. Write in pencil or ink?

I'm not sure it matters much as long as you avoid inking in firmly before you have worked out both the definition and wordplay. There is nothing worse than being held up for a long time by an incorrect entry made in haste. A thoughtful Christmas present bought for me some years ago was the delightful compromise of a pen with ink that could be erased.

2. Empty grid: how to start?

You have a puzzle in front of you which looks totally impossible – maybe you start to feel inadequate but remember that most puzzles, by accident or design, give you at least one clue to get you going and all you have to do is find it! It may be a **hidden** clue; after all, the letters of the solution are there facing you as part of the clue. So scan the clues for a **hidden** indicator. But supposing the mean setter this time gives you no **hidden** clues. What should you do when there appears to be no way in? There are various points:

- It is rare for there to be no **anagram** clue, so why not scan for an **anagram** indicator? Do inspect the longest words as they are more likely to be clued by anagrams than shorter ones. Once found, the letters are there as with **hidden** clues, waiting to be unscrambled.
- Try to spot an obvious definition. One experienced solver told me he can see a definition nearly always instantly – but that was after 40 years of solving!
- At this stage it's a good idea to find a clue that seems to be within your areas of interests or expertise. For example, in my

case it is always comforting to spot clues which seem to have a musical, political or a sporting component. Of course I have to be aware that I may be being led up the garden path.

- Look for short solutions of up to five letters because there are fewer words that can fit the space indicated. While it's rewarding to get the 15-letter word at 1 across immediately, that is rare.
- Try the compound phrases that are present in most puzzles. As covered earlier, the likes of 3,2,4 and 4,4,1,4 are a gift in the sense that the shorter lengths can often be guessed.
- Keep in mind that the tense of the clue and the solution must be the same. So look for plurals, -*ing* and -*ed* in potential definitions. Try to formulate an answer from this but beware inking in such endings in error.
- Try to find proper names and ask yourself why they may have been included. Getting into the setter's mind in this respect and in other aspects of cryptic clues can be rewarding.

TOP TIP – WHERE TO START?

More than one solver I know considers that you should look at the bottom right hand corner first as the setter, having written the clues in order from 1 across, is tired by the time the bottom of the grid is reached. Hence the clues are easier than elsewhere. Based on my own setting process, I'm sceptical about this but, nonetheless, if that approach helps you to gain the confidence essential to solving, I'd say stick with it.

---

3. How to continue?

After one clue is solved, where next? Try building on the most promising (i.e. less common) of the intersecting letters you have available. Don't attempt clues for which you have no letters until you become convinced you can make no progress with the letters you have. Crossword solving is a process of gains being built up cumulatively and, at this early stage, there may or may not be gains to make.

Try a little harder to crack clues that yield the best follow-on letters, e.g. those running across the top and down the sides. As one of my correspondents put it, first letters are usually worth a lot. Also when more letters are available, you may find that you can anticipate solutions from letter patterns such as -*ation*, -*ive*, -*ally* and the like.

ARE SOME GRIDS EASIER THAN OTHERS?

Those in which the highest number of initial letters of answers are potentially available to help with other answers are likely to prove best for new solvers. This is shown in these two below, the bottom one in principle being an easier solve.

6. The Knowledge

> 'Crosswords are notoriously worked at by quite humble members of society.'
> *Times* Leader 1928, referring to the USA

Some items which are common to many puzzles and which, after a time, you will take for granted are covered in this next chapter. Just as it takes London cabbies some years to acquire all the information needed for their task, so it is with crosswords. What follows is a randomly ordered set of items that I hope helps you along the way to becoming a solver of excellence.

1. Numerals

Numerals, chiefly roman, are common so in alphabetical order you will find:

eleven	xi	**hundred**	c
fifty	l	**hundred and fifty**	cl
fifty-one	li	**nine**	ix
five	v	**six**	vi
five hundred	d	**ten**	x
four	iv	**thousand**	m and k

Numbers such as eighteen (XVIII) are unlikely to be met for obvious reasons.

2. Compass points

Equally common are compass points. The abbreviations for north, south, east and west and their two-letter combinations need no listing here but look for *point* or *quarter* which can do duty for any of the four. This can involve testing each in turn to see whether it yields part of, or the full, solution. Very occasionally you may need to think of three-letter compass points, as in this clue:

SANDWICH CLUE: Wind bearing round spit (7)

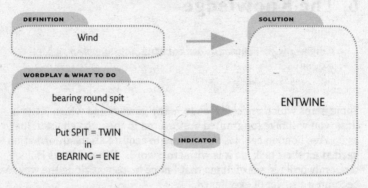

DEFINITION		SOLUTION
Wind		
WORDPLAY & WHAT TO DO		
bearing round spit	**INDICATOR**	ENTWINE
Put SPIT = TWIN in BEARING = ENE		

N,E,W and S are Bridge players too (see 13 below).

3. Foreign languages
Some knowledge of foreign languages is needed but only of simple words in the more familiar, usually European, languages. Thus German articles *der, die* or *das*; French ones *le, la* or *l'*; and Spanish *el, la* or *los*; and the equivalent indefinite articles in these languages are regarded as fair game, as are common French words such as *oui, rue* and *et*. Look out for misleading indications of Frenchness such as *Nice, Angers* and *Nancy*. Here's a more straightforward example:

ADDITIVE CLUE: See some of the French weep (6)

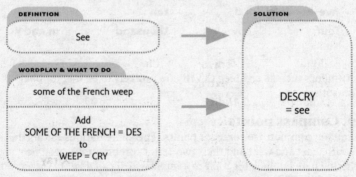

DEFINITION	SOLUTION
See	
WORDPLAY & WHAT TO DO	
some of the French weep	DESCRY = see
Add SOME OF THE FRENCH = DES to WEEP = CRY	

4. Military types

Military types can appear in their abbreviated form as below but also more generally as soldier(s), officer(s), rank, unit(s) and the like.

American soldier	GI	gunners	RA
artillery	RA	lieutenant	LT
colonel	COL	officer	NCO, OC
engineers	RE	other ranks	OR
general	GEN	volunteers	TA

5. Rivers

Rivers feature in crosswords as the abbreviation *R* and also, because of their size, the *Po*, *Exe* or *Dee*. As always it's trial and error that unlocks which particular one is required. Another more esoteric expression of *river* is *flower* (see Chapter 10, page 106).

6. Alphabets

A brief recall of some alphabets may come in handy. In particular:

GREEK LETTERS

beta	chi	delta	eta
iota	mu	nu	phi
pi	psi	rho	tau
xi			

NATO

alpha	bravo	Charlie	delta
echo	foxtrot	golf	hotel
India	Juliet	kilo	lima
Mike	November	Oscar	papa
Quebec	Romeo	sierra	tango
uniform	victor	whiskey	X-ray
Yankee	Zulu		

7. Cricket terms

Though many sports and games do appear in crosswords (golf and tennis perhaps more than soccer or rugby), the quaint often short terms and frequent abbreviations used in cricket are a gift to setters. Non-cricket loving participants on my workshops tell me this is a cause of frustration, so here are the cricket abbreviations likely to be encountered:

bowled	B	maiden	M
bye	B	one-day international	ODI
caught	C or CT	run or runs	R
duck	O	run out	RO
eleven	XI	stumped	ST
fifty	L	wicket	W
hundred	C	wide	W
length	L		

In addition, these cricket terms are common: batting (IN), cricket side (LEG and ON), extra (BYE), ton (C = one hundred) and deliveries (OVER).

8. Chemical elements

Remember your chemical elements? Here are those most beloved of setters:

arsenic	AS	calcium	CA
copper	CU	gold	AU
helium	HE	hydrogen	H
iron	FE	lead	PB
nitrogen	N	potassium	K
silver	AG	tin	SN
tungsten	W		

The following wonderfully misleading effort uses one of these:

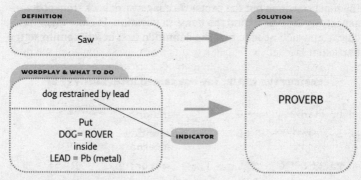

SANDWICH CLUE: Saw dog restrained by lead (7)

DEFINITION
Saw

SOLUTION
PROVERB

WORDPLAY & WHAT TO DO
dog restrained by lead

INDICATOR

Put
DOG= ROVER
inside
LEAD = Pb (metal)

9. The City of London

Though now effectively split across several postal areas including Canary Wharf, in crosswords it is still thought of as the old Square Mile; actually not even all of it (EC2), just EC for City or The City in wordplay, as below in a clue with a debatable sentiment:

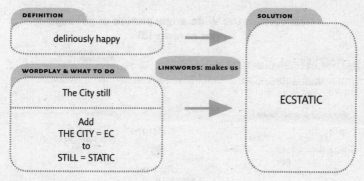

ADDITIVE CLUE: The City still makes us deliriously happy (8)

DEFINITION
deliriously happy

SOLUTION

LINKWORDS: makes us

WORDPLAY & WHAT TO DO
The City still

ECSTATIC

Add
THE CITY = EC
to
STILL = STATIC

10. Chess

Chess notations that appear are: bishop (B), king (K), knight (N), pawn (P), queen (Q), rook (R). In addition, the word *board* in a clue may well be referring to chess.

11. Names

In part of the wordplay, names of boys and girls, arguably unfairly, can be indicated by the terse *boy* or *girl*, etc. Probably *Ed*, *Ted*, *Di* and *Ian* (the latter surprisingly reckoned often to be a Scotsman) are the most common but the best advice is to work back from other aspects of the clue to find the name in question. In this rather hard clue, you would need to find the definition first before coming to the particular lad:

ADDITIVE CLUE: Toy boy talked incessantly (7,2)

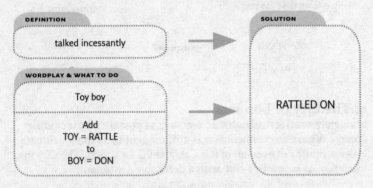

DEFINITION

talked incessantly

SOLUTION

WORDPLAY & WHAT TO DO

Toy boy

Add
TOY = RATTLE
to
BOY = DON

RATTLED ON

... and here's a less common name in an enjoyable clue:

SANDWICH CLUE: Wide-angle picture of girl kept by her parents (8)

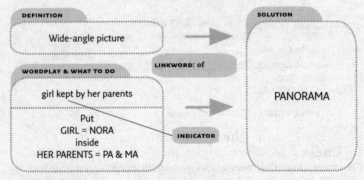

DEFINITION

Wide-angle picture

SOLUTION

LINKWORD: of

WORDPLAY & WHAT TO DO

girl kept by her parents

Put
GIRL = NORA
inside
HER PARENTS = PA & MA

INDICATOR

PANORAMA

12. Setters

Despite the fact that many newspapers do not reveal the names of their setters, he or she does appear in clues. This can be as *Yours Truly*, *I* or *me* within wordplay. Here's an example:

SANDWICH CLUE: Rather restricting the setter? I don't care! (8)

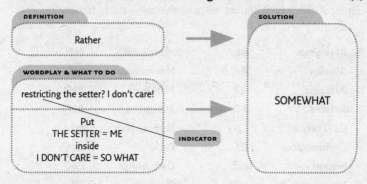

DEFINITION

Rather

SOLUTION

WORDPLAY & WHAT TO DO

restricting the setter? I don't care!

Put
THE SETTER = ME
inside
I DON'T CARE = SO WHAT

INDICATOR

SOMEWHAT

13. Bridge

Bridge notation features in terms of north, south, east and west in abbreviated form and this can extend to Bridge partners as here:

ADDITIVE CLUE:
Heart led by opponents at bridge – play again! (6)

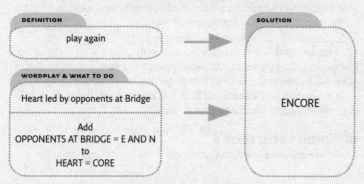

DEFINITION

play again

SOLUTION

WORDPLAY & WHAT TO DO

Heart led by opponents at Bridge

Add
OPPONENTS AT BRIDGE = E AND N
to
HEART = CORE

ENCORE

14. Accents and other punctuation

Accents, hyphens and apostrophes are of course included in clue sentences but, by convention, they are not entered into the grid. For example, *its* and *it's* in clues would be entered in the same way (as the former) in the grid.

15. Some US states
Those states which appear more than others are in the box below:

Alabama	AL	Minnesota	MN
Alaska	AK	Mississippi	MS
Arizona	AZ	Missouri	MO
Arkansas	AR	Montana	MT
California	CA	Nebraska	NE
Connecticut	CT	Ohio	OH
Maine	ME	Oklahoma	OK
Maryland	MD	Oregon	OR
Massachusetts	MA	Washington	WA
Michigan	MI		

16. Workers
The word *worker* could be a reference to the human kind but, more likely, it will be a synonym for *ant* or *bee*.

17. On board
Phrases such as *on board* can be related to chess, e.g. men or pieces, or ships. In addition, SS (= steam ship) can be exploited in wording such as *on board* in a **sandwich** clue. Thus a word like *train* may be inserted between *s* and *s* to give *strains*.

18. Some Latin terms
These are perhaps the most common:

and so on	ETC	present day	AD
afternoon	PM	see	V
approximately, about	CA	that is or that's	IE
morning	AM	thus	SIC

7. Ten Things to Consider When Stuck

'Congratulations to all who completed this puzzle which was printed with the wrong grid.'
Sunday Telegraph

Even the best solvers get held up or seriously stuck at times. Here are ten reasons why you may also hit a wall, with suggestions as to how to make a breakthrough.

1. Check for a wrong entry

The first point to consider is whether you have made a mistake in an earlier entry. Once a word is 'inked' into the grid, you naturally become reluctant to consider other possibilities for the solution in question.

Even experienced hands like me trip up by inserting incorrect answers into the grid too quickly, for example without having matched wordplay to definition or vice versa. It's maddening to spend a long time working from wrong assumptions so do check this possibility first.

2. Ignore the surface reading

The vital fact to keep in mind is that the setter's aim is to produce a sentence that appears to mean one thing but may well, and usually does, mean something totally different. In the very best clues, this is achieved by the creation of a highly misleading image. The solver's response is to enjoy the image but ignore it – the solution may come out after a close examination of each word rather than appreciation of the scenario presented. Try not to miss the subtlety of a clue, but only after being sure of the solution.

3. Look carefully again and consider each word in the clue

Cunning setters find ways of using familiar combinations and juxtapositions which require splitting before any progress can be made. Consider the clue below. You may well have got stuck on this until you realised that the two words *British Isles* have to be separated to uncover the definition.

SANDWICH CLUE: Ambassador travels round British Isles (8)

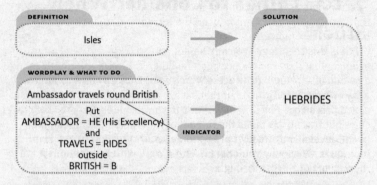

DEFINITION

Isles

WORDPLAY & WHAT TO DO

Ambassador travels round British

Put
AMBASSADOR = HE (His Excellency)
and
TRAVELS = RIDES
outside
BRITISH = B

INDICATOR

SOLUTION

HEBRIDES

TOP TIP – PARTS OF SPEECH
Use of misleading parts of speech is a strong feature. Participants in my workshops are misled time and again by this and my suggestion is that, when temporarily stuck, you reconsider carefully every word of the clue which could have an alternative part of speech.

4. Endings
Based on a definition in the past tense, you may have pencilled or, even worse, inked in the ending *-ed* when the actual solution is, say, *caught* or *known*. Similar problems can arise after putting in an *-s* or an *-ing* – sensible practice, usually, but needing reconsideration when you are stuck.

5. Take a break to do something else
This is the most popular tip of all from solvers. Doing the washing up or taking the dog for a walk has the most liberating effect on the blocked crossword mind. You may find that this extends to getting a solution the next morning – or even during the night.

6. Ring the help line
If you cannot wait that long, the solution to the current day's puzzle can be obtained via a paid phone call to the number shown at the foot of each day's puzzle.

7. 'Cheat' via electronic aids and the internet

Crosswords are rarely a competition so you make your own rules as regards using electronic aids. Using dictionaries to confirm a solution is just common sense; going further to root out a solution electronically is now much easier than hitherto as word completion tools, especially prevalent now on the internet, virtually guarantee finding tricky answers.

But is this cheating? Typically half of my students will be firmly against what they see as cheating; the other half see it differently as a means of shortening a process which would anyway have led to the answer later. The ultimate, if that's what you want, is a programme called Crossword Maestro. It reckons to solve a high percentage of clues but that surely takes the fun out of the whole thing. Incidentally, the developer claims his programme knows over 4000 anagram indicators. Without going that far, and if conventional dictionary/thesaurus hunting has failed or is too time-consuming, you can try a word completion tool. Some of these are listed in Chapter 13.

You can also seek help with a particular clue via a website such as www.answerbank.com. This, I'm told, nearly always finds someone kind enough to give an answer. Finally you can type a clue into Google and see what comes up. Impressively, on a random test, this threw up the answer to six of seven clues from different newspapers!

8. Consult the blog

See Chapter 13. Not only does this usually give the answer on the day of the publication but it helpfully gives the wordplay or an explanation.

9. Phone a friend

It's remarkable how two or more brains working on a clue can come up with answers much more effectively than one.

10. Ask the Cluru

If you still need help in understanding why a solution is the answer to what was published, there are services available for this too. One such is for Crossword Club members (also see Chapter 12) offered by the Cluru (Clue Guru, currently myself). It is noticeable with the advent of Google and blogs that requests are fewer than they once were and the resource now primarily helps the diminishing few who do not use computers. Sometimes queries refer to puzzles which have bothered people for years. In one instance a 2004 query related to an *Observer* 1939 puzzle!

PART 2

MASTERING THE FINER POINTS

8. Finer Points: by Clue Type

Please do not be put off tackling cryptics by this and the next chapter which are largely concerned with those at the upper end of the spectrum. If you have successfully absorbed the previous chapters, there is every reason why you should make good progress with most of the crosswords you try. So, many readers may best be advised to skip to Chapter 10 for the time being.

> 'The nicest thing about a crossword is that you know there's a solution. A crossword is an unusual puzzle in that you can derive enjoyment from it, even if you cannot complete it entirely (provided that the setter has shown wit, wisdom and elegance).'
>
> Stephen Sondheim, who introduced Americans to the cryptic crossword puzzle,
> *Secrets of the Setters*

We move up from basics to consider the finer points of clues and puzzles. The charts from now on have wordplay analysis as an explanation rather than an indication of what to do.

Assuming that you wish to go along with the optimism of the above quotation, I'll start with the finer points associated with clue types, and then those that apply generally to all clues.

1. The anagram clue: finer points
From now on, we will indicate which words form the **anagram fodder** by an asterisk (*).

Anagram fodder: which letters? (1)
Some crosswords require you to find an interim solution and then make an anagram of that. Called an **indirect anagram**, the practice is almost extinct, as it should be. However, where there is a unique interim solution such as *omicron* (*pi*'s predecessor in the Greek alphabet), you may see a clue such as the one overleaf.

ANAGRAM CLUE 1: It's crazy changing what comes before pi (7)

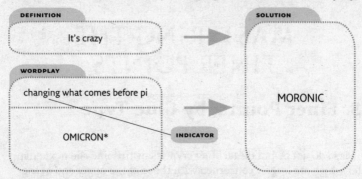

DEFINITION

It's crazy

WORDPLAY

changing what comes before pi

OMICRON*

INDICATOR

SOLUTION

MORONIC

TOP TIP – ANAGRAM FREQUENCY

It is rare for there to be no anagrams in a cryptic puzzle and equally rare to find more than about eight in total, with two-part anagrams counting as one whole-word anagram.

Anagram fodder: which letters? (2)

The anagram fodder can be part of a hyphenated word, as here:

ANAGRAM CLUE: Aspiring to achieve first in Wimbledon, double-faulted (5-2)

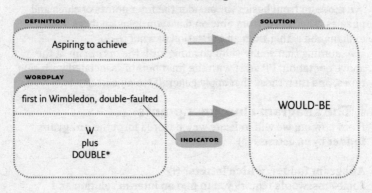

DEFINITION

Aspiring to achieve

WORDPLAY

first in Wimbledon, double-faulted

W
plus
DOUBLE*

INDICATOR

SOLUTION

WOULD-BE

Position of the indicator

While anagrams are always indicated in one of the many ways already covered in Chapter 3, the position of the indicator is not always immediately next to the **anagram fodder**. In the clue below, a letter has to be deducted before the anagram can be unscrambled:

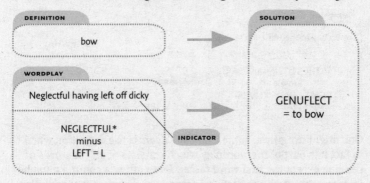

2. The sandwich clue: finer points

The basis of this very common clue type, something inside something else, is often the technique that delays solvers, so its tricks and quirks should repay study.

Its use in any one clue may be in conjunction with, say, an **anagram**, and be indicated by a less than obvious indicator. In the following example, the indicator *stop* is used in its sense of *block* or *plug* (perhaps more normally *stop up*):

SANDWICH CLUE: **Nothing stops Chelsea playing tie (8)**

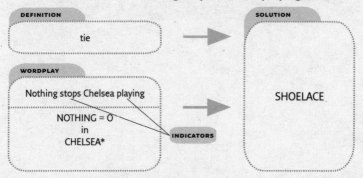

Sometimes the element to be sandwiched is difficult to disentangle, as in this clue, which we looked at before in another context:

SANDWICH CLUE: Rather restricting the setter? I don't care! (8)

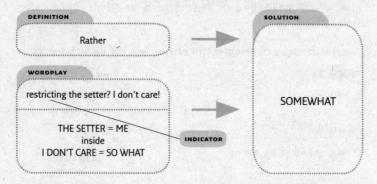

DEFINITION
Rather

WORDPLAY
restricting the setter? I don't care!

THE SETTER = ME
inside
I DON'T CARE = SO WHAT

INDICATOR

SOLUTION
SOMEWHAT

One might initially assume that *I don't care* is the definition when in fact it is part of the wordplay which consists of all the words of the clue except the first word *rather*. As so often, a comma must be imagined between the first and second words before you can solve the clue.

> **TOP TIP – 'HIDDEN' VS. 'SANDWICH' CLUES**
> I find workshop participants do confuse **hidden** and **sandwich** clues, partly because their indicators are similar. The difference is that in **hidden** clues, the word to be found is contained exactly (albeit with intervening punctuation sometimes) within the clue sentence. In **sandwich** clues, the solution word is to be constructed by the solver from the separate elements available.

The sandwich can be formed with a kind of reverse construction, as here:

SANDWICH CLUE: **Fall in love? On the contrary, wilt (5)**

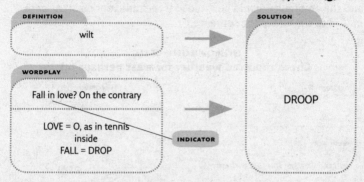

DEFINITION
wilt

SOLUTION
DROOP

WORDPLAY
Fall in love? On the contrary

LOVE = O, as in tennis
inside
FALL = DROP

INDICATOR

Here is a very misleading and tricky sandwich, boasting an unusual indicator and the word *for* that looks as if it is a linkword but isn't:

SANDWICH CLUE: **Composer of lines for capital city (8)**

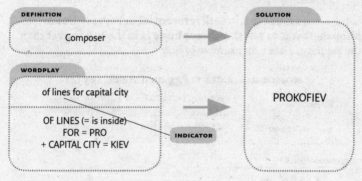

DEFINITION
Composer

SOLUTION
PROKOFIEV

WORDPLAY
of lines for capital city

OF LINES (= is inside)
FOR = PRO
+ CAPITAL CITY = KIEV

INDICATOR

The message again is that study of each word individually pays off.

3. The homophone clue: finer points

In the best clue-writing, you should be left in no doubt in a **homophone** clue as to which word is the solution and which the wordplay. For example, the solution to the next clue could be *rain* or *rein* and the ambiguity would be avoided if the indicator *reported* were moved to the end of the sentence.

HOMOPHONE CLUE:
Check reported weather forecast perhaps (4)

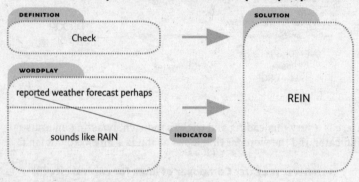

Some crosswords contain **self-referential** or **reverse homophones**; that is to say, the **homophone** is in the clue, rather than the solution. Here's an example of one:

HOMOPHONE CLUE: Egg on a steak, say (4)

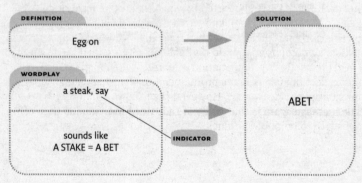

This is another **reverse homophone** which has the attraction of using alphabet letters in a novel way:

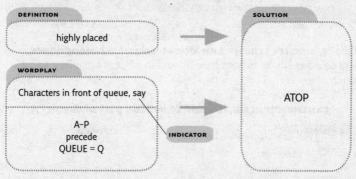

HOMOPHONE CLUE: **Characters in front of queue, say highly placed (4)**

DEFINITION
highly placed

SOLUTION
ATOP

WORDPLAY
Characters in front of queue, say

A–P
precede
QUEUE = Q

INDICATOR

TOP TIP – THE LETTER 'U'
A long-established extension of **reverse homophones** is that *you* may be used as a proxy for *you say* to give the letter *u* in part of the wordplay.

You may be stuck on a **homophone** clue because its sound to you is not the same as your pronunciation. The test for setters is whether the pronunciation is supported by one of the reference dictionaries (see Chapter 13) and I well know that setters receive complaints on this subject. Correspondents (especially from Scotland) clearly dislike a homophone they do not relate to, especially if the inference is that the setter's pronunciation is 'correct'. Ideally the indicator will reflect the fact that the pronunciation is not universal, as in, for example, *some may say*. However, the teaching point here is that solvers may occasionally need to be a little imaginative in their approach to homophone clues.

Finally, beware of clues which look as if they are **homophones** – you could easily be misled here by *said* in what is actually a **sandwich** clue:

SANDWICH CLUE: It's said to include part of circuit (7)

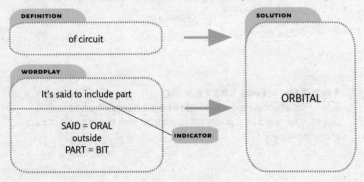

4. The hidden clue: finer points

The indicator may be at the end of the clue sentence as in the example below, in which the interpretation should be that a synonym of *zip* is being *employed* by the letters that follow it:

HIDDEN CLUE: **Zip fastener gymnast employs (6)**

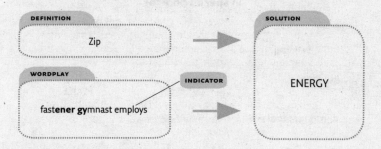

Also in a more difficult category, the solution can be spread over more than two words:

HIDDEN CLUE: **Wine to some extent features in a taverna (8)**

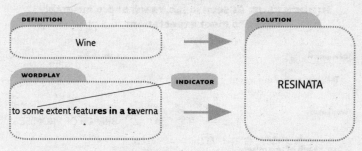

The letters concealed may have to be reversed before the solution is discovered, as overleaf:

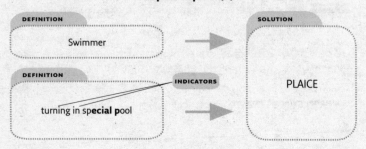

HIDDEN AND REVERSAL CLUE: Swimmer turning in special pool (6)

DEFINITION

Swimmer

DEFINITION

INDICATORS

turning in sp**ecial p**ool

SOLUTION

PLAICE

You should be on the lookout for very long and well-concealed solutions. This next wonderful effort must be just about the longest **hidden** clue that has appeared in a crossword:

HIDDEN CLUE: As seen in jab, reach of pro miserably failing to meet expectations (6,2,7)

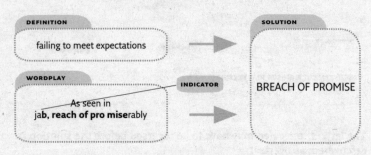

DEFINITION

failing to meet expectations

WORDPLAY

INDICATOR

As seen in
ja**b, reach of pro mise**rably

SOLUTION

BREACH OF PROMISE

TOP TIP – HIDDEN CLUE FREQUENCY

Because they are considered to be the easiest type, there may be no **hidden** clue in any one daily puzzle and rarely more than two or three. I refer to 15 by 15 square puzzles; there may well be proportionately more in jumbo-style puzzles.

Finally, for clues requiring the selection of alternate letters, it may be that not all the hidden letters form the whole solution. This is a combination of a **hidden** with an **additive** clue to demonstrate that point:

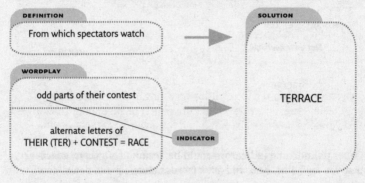

HIDDEN AND ADDITIVE CLUE: **From which spectators watch odd parts of their contest (7)**

DEFINITION

From which spectators watch

SOLUTION

WORDPLAY

odd parts of their contest

alternate letters of
THEIR (TER) + CONTEST = RACE

INDICATOR

TERRACE

5. The reversal clue: finer points

Clues can be made up of reversals of more than one word. This one, with its nicely misleading definition, has two reversals:

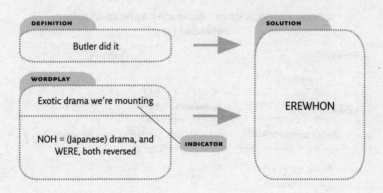

REVERSAL CLUE (DOWN CLUE): **Exotic drama we're mounting – Butler did it (7)**

DEFINITION

Butler did it

SOLUTION

WORDPLAY

Exotic drama we're mounting

NOH = (Japanese) drama, and
WERE, both reversed

INDICATOR

EREWHON

Also in this category of clue, we include **palindromes**. Here's an elegant example:

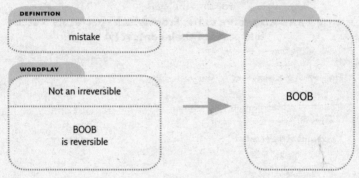

REVERSAL CLUE: Not an irreversible mistake (4)

DEFINITION
mistake

WORDPLAY
Not an irreversible

BOOB
is reversible

BOOB

Other palindrome indicators could be: *looking both ways*, *whichever way you look at it*, *back and forth* (across clue), *up and down* (down clue).

6. The letter switch clue: finer points
The first example is similar to that in Chapter 3 where the letter to be switched is within the clue itself, whereas the second example is harder as the word to be manipulated must be found before the switch can be made:

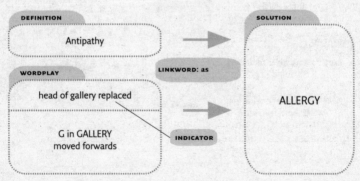

LETTER SWITCH CLUE: Antipathy as head of gallery replaced (7)

DEFINITION
Antipathy

SOLUTION

LINKWORD: as

WORDPLAY
head of gallery replaced

G in GALLERY
moved forwards

INDICATOR

ALLERGY

This second clue is also tougher because the switch indication is *for*, more usually a linkword:

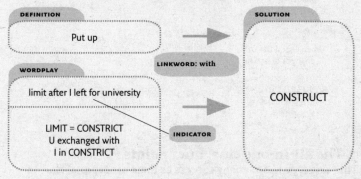

LETTER SWITCH CLUE: Put up with limit after I left for university (9)

DEFINITION

Put up

LINKWORD: with

WORDPLAY

limit after I left for university

LIMIT = CONSTRICT
U exchanged with
I in CONSTRICT

INDICATOR

SOLUTION

CONSTRUCT

This use of abbreviations (for example, *good for nothing* would mean *G* replacing *O* in one word to make another) is not uncommon. Another type of letter switch is shown next.

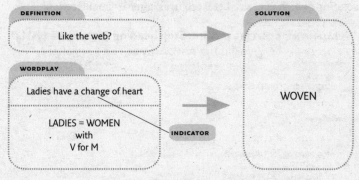

LETTER SWITCH CLUE: Like the web? Ladies have a change of heart (5)

DEFINITION

Like the web?

WORDPLAY

Ladies have a change of heart

LADIES = WOMEN
with
V for M

INDICATOR

SOLUTION

WOVEN

Finally for the next example, a change of direction may be required as in this nice clue which requires you to switch your thoughts from military matters to boiled eggs:

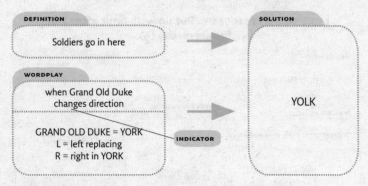

LETTER SWITCH CLUE: Soldiers go in here when grand old duke changes direction (4)

DEFINITION

Soldiers go in here

WORDPLAY

when Grand Old Duke changes direction

GRAND OLD DUKE = YORK
L = left replacing
R = right in YORK

INDICATOR

SOLUTION

YOLK

7. The all-in-one clue: finer points

This clue type has as many subsets as there are types of clue. In other words, the wordplay (remember: always the same as the definition, hence the term **all-in-one**) can take the form of an **anagram**, **additive** or any other sort. Indeed it can even be a combination of these. Here are some examples:

All-in-one additive clue:

The example below shows the clue type at its most concise and the solution (which is a verb here) requires careful consideration:

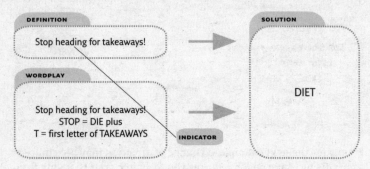

ALL-IN-ONE ADDITIVE CLUE: Stop heading for takeaways! (4)

DEFINITION

Stop heading for takeaways!

WORDPLAY

Stop heading for takeaways!
STOP = DIE plus
T = first letter of TAKEAWAYS

INDICATOR

SOLUTION

DIET

All-in-one anagram:

The most common type of all-in-one clue is the **anagram**. Here's a great one which has a letter to be inserted in the **anagram fodder**:

ALL-IN-ONE ANAGRAM AND SANDWICH CLUE:
What's outlined arbitrarily around origin in Greenwich? (9)

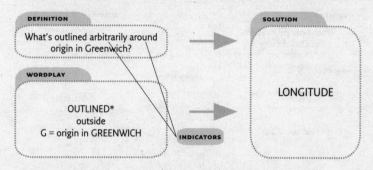

All-in-one anagram and takeaway:

This involves an **anagram** and **takeaway** but is still eminently solvable – if you think comma after *actors*:

ALL-IN-ONE ANAGRAM AND TAKEAWAY CLUE:
What could give actors no end of cachet? (5)

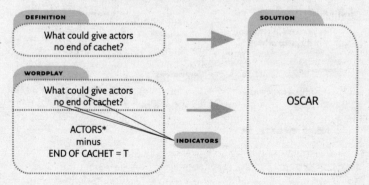

All-in-one hidden:
The wordplay can be concealed neatly, as here, albeit that the answer word may have been replaced by a rucksack:

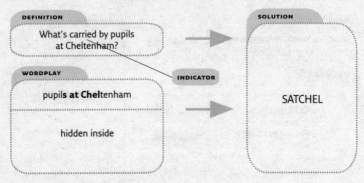

ALL-IN-ONE HIDDEN CLUE: What's carried by pupils at Cheltenham? (7)

DEFINITION	SOLUTION
What's carried by pupils at Cheltenham?	

WORDPLAY	INDICATOR
pupil**s at Chel**tenham	
hidden inside	SATCHEL

All-in-one hidden and reversal:
The wordplay can also be hidden and reversed with a plural definition:

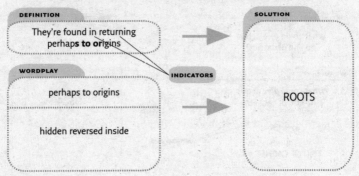

ALL-IN-ONE HIDDEN AND REVERSAL CLUE: They're found in returning perhaps to origins (5)

DEFINITION	SOLUTION
They're found in returning perhaps **to or**igins	

WORDPLAY	INDICATORS
perhaps to origins	
hidden reversed inside	ROOTS

All-in-one sandwich and anagram:
Here, by the way, the question mark is needed as the solution is only one example of what a shaking duster might collect:

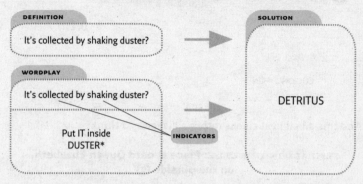

ALL-IN-ONE SANDWICH AND ANAGRAM CLUE:
It's collected by shaking duster? (8)

DEFINITION
It's collected by shaking duster?

SOLUTION

WORDPLAY
It's collected by shaking duster?

Put IT inside
DUSTER*

INDICATORS

DETRITUS

IS THE ALL-IN-ONE CLUE THE MOST SATISFYING?
Setters and judges of clue-writing contests tend to regard this sort of clue as the pinnacle of clue-writing and it's true that all these examples boast something special with their coincidence of definition and wordplay. However, the **all-in-one** is not necessarily considered so highly by the solvers I ask; their preference is a clue with a highly misleading image and a pleasingly delayed penny-dropping. In addition, the **all-in-one** may reveal its charms too quickly, especially in the case of the subset discussed next.

There is a variation on the **all-in-one** clue in which the definition is extended by wordplay into a whole sentence. We could think of it as **partial** or a **semi all-in-one**. Solving this type of clue is in principle easier because of the extended definition. Here's one example:

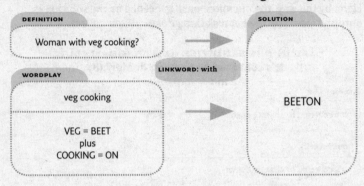

SEMI ALL-IN-ONE CLUE: Woman with veg cooking? (6)

DEFINITION

Woman with veg cooking?

WORDPLAY

veg cooking

VEG = BEET
plus
COOKING = ON

LINKWORD: with

SOLUTION

BEETON

And this albeit neat clue is rather a giveaway, I think:

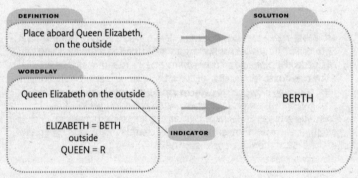

SEMI ALL-IN-ONE CLUE: Place aboard Queen Elizabeth, on the outside (5)

DEFINITION

Place aboard Queen Elizabeth, on the outside

WORDPLAY

Queen Elizabeth on the outside

ELIZABETH = BETH
outside
QUEEN = R

INDICATOR

SOLUTION

BERTH

8. The additive clue: finer points

Some crosswords, notably *The Times*, follow a convention established over many years in making a distinction between the across and down position in **additive** clues.

This concerns the word *on* which, as a linkword, means *after* in an across clue and *before* in a down clue, as set out next.

For across clues:

The part that comes first in the solution is placed second in the wordplay. For example, here the *great bloke* (*top cock*) comes after the *s* (*for pole*):

ADDITIVE CLUE (ACROSS): Great bloke on pole, the main controller (8)

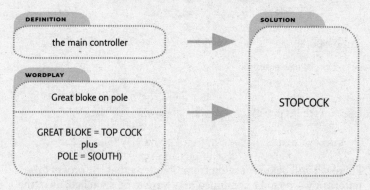

DEFINITION

the main controller

WORDPLAY

Great bloke on pole

GREAT BLOKE = TOP COCK
plus
POLE = S(OUTH)

SOLUTION

STOPCOCK

For down clues:

In down clues the parts keep the order of the clue sentence, as with the *was* preceding the *sail* = *canvas* in this:

ADDITIVE CLUE (DOWN): Festive occasion was put on canvas (7)

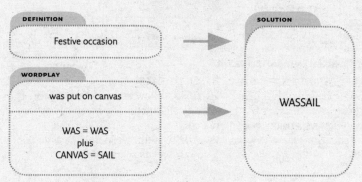

DEFINITION

Festive occasion

WORDPLAY

was put on canvas

WAS = WAS
plus
CANVAS = SAIL

SOLUTION

WASSAIL

Sometimes the solution word can be broken down into separate parts to form the wordplay. Solving these clues is often a question of working from the definition back to the wordplay:

ADDITIVE CLUE: Cold display unit for seafood (11)

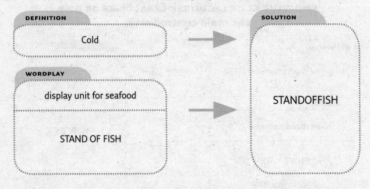

Finally, it will bear repetition from Chapter 3 that the order of the letters or words to be combined may have to be switched, as in the next clue:

ADDITIVE CLUE: Vegetable presented with dessert? That's a bloomer (5,3)

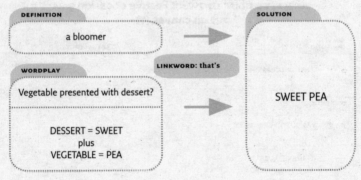

9. The cryptic definition clue: finer points

The more instinctive solver finds this clue one of the easiest; others like me find it the hardest and my practice, once I have recognized the type, is to leave it till later when some solution letters are available. This is especially so when the information given is minimal, as here:

CRYPTIC DEFINITION CLUE: Decline in need of a fall (3,5)

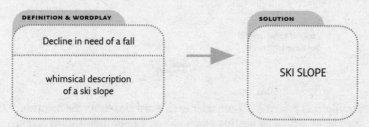

This type of wordplay can extend to two misleading words in the clue, as in this example:

CRYPTIC DEFINITION CLUE: What's made only to snap in bits? (7,6)

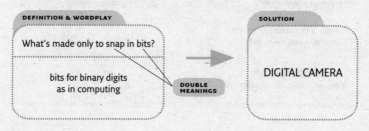

Occasionally the clue-writer manages to be exceptionally cryptic as here where no fewer than three words have misleading surface meanings:

CRYPTIC DEFINITION CLUE: It's bound to be upheld by those in service (4-4)

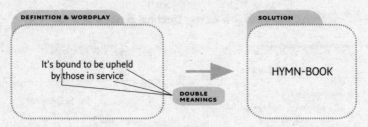

Finally, it is essential to consider each word closely as the solution may be unlocked by putting emphasis on a seemingly unimportant part of the clue, as here:

CRYPTIC DEFINITION CLUE: Help with mental problems one can never get (5,7)

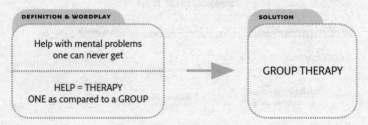

10. The double definition clue: finer points

While these can be recognized from their brevity when there are only two words side by side, they can be longer and harder to spot:

DOUBLE DEFINITION CLUE: A lot of criminals go north of the border (4)

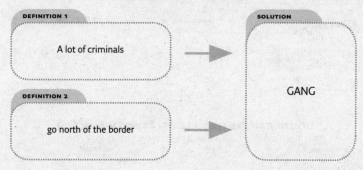

Also note that there may be one of several possible linkwords between the two or more definitions. *For*, *in* and *is* are three linkword examples in these clues:

DOUBLE DEFINITION CLUE: Responsibility for tax (4)

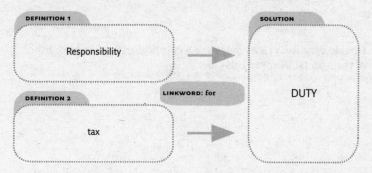

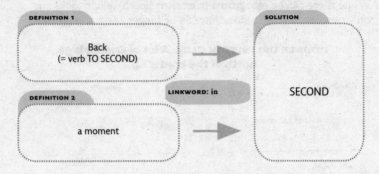

DOUBLE DEFINITION CLUE: Back in a moment (6)

DEFINITION 1

Back
(= verb TO SECOND)

LINKWORD: in

DEFINITION 2

a moment

SOLUTION

SECOND

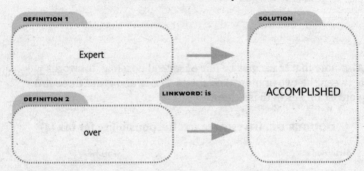

DOUBLE DEFINITION CLUE: Expert is over (12)

DEFINITION 1

Expert

LINKWORD: is

DEFINITION 2

over

SOLUTION

ACCOMPLISHED

Double definition clues may have a cryptic element in one or other of their parts. Witness this clue:

**DOUBLE DEFINITION CLUE: Comfortable job
for a boring person (4-2-2)**

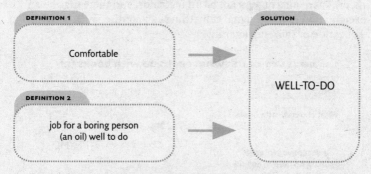

Finally, an example of three definitions which exploit a word with multiple meanings. There is no special tip for finding your way through this ingenious and mischievous wording other than to note that it contains nothing that looks like an indicator of another clue type:

**TRIPLE DEFINITION CLUE: Run some ginger group
of similar people (4)**

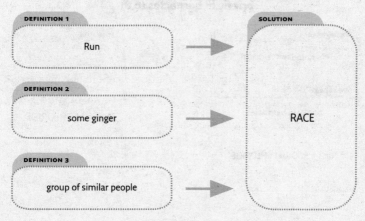

11. The novelty clue: finer points

By their very nature, these clues defy generalized advice on solving them. There may or may not be an indicator, and there may be an exclamation mark to signal something extraordinary. Otherwise it's a question of thinking laterally:

NOVELTY CLUE: What cooks do with books (5)

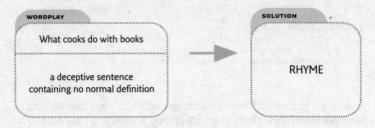

The next example is a rare but agreeable case of something concealed as an abbreviation (NaCl) within part of the wordplay which, unabbreviated, gives the solution:

NOVELTY CLUE: It's found in the ocean and briefly in barnacles (6,8)

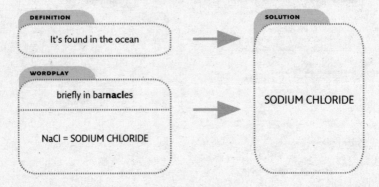

In the next example, the clue-writer exploits the repetition of letters (*S,E,A,T*) within the solution, and incidentally finds a one-word definition (*calm*) in a different part of speech to that of the solution. The message is: ignore the definitional part of speech.

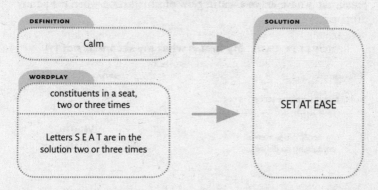

NOVELTY CLUE: Calm constituents in a seat, two or three times (3,2,4)

DEFINITION		SOLUTION
Calm	→	
WORDPLAY		SET AT EASE
constituents in a seat, two or three times	→	
Letters S E A T are in the solution two or three times		

Next, you must split the solution into two parts and imagine it as a slogan supporting the Queen.

NOVELTY CLUE: Servant's anti-republican slogan? (8)

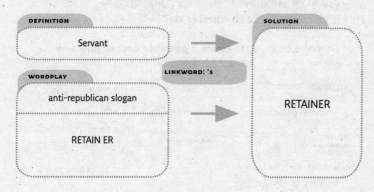

DEFINITION		SOLUTION
Servant	→	
WORDPLAY	LINKWORD: 's	RETAINER
anti-republican slogan	→	
RETAIN ER		

Here is a really 'off-the-wall' clue which, strictly speaking, is defective in that it lacks a definition. However, it's fun and would presumably have led to a warm glow of satisfaction when the penny dropped:

NOVELTY CLUE: **My first is what my second is not (7)**

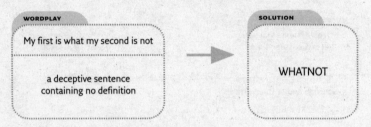

Under this heading we can include clues which use the verbal twisting of William Archibald Spooner. He was an Anglican clergyman and Warden of New College, Oxford, whose nervous manner led him to utter many slips of the tongue, notably involving comic reversals such as Queer old Dean for Dear old Queen.
This is an example of a clue in this style:

NOVELTY CLUE: **Lowest possible cost of jam and cereal for Spooner (7,5)**

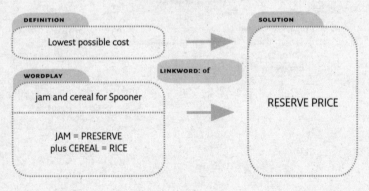

Here is a favoured clue that is perhaps more of a riddle than a clue:

**NOVELTY CLUE: If one cold toe is numb,
two must be _____ (4,6)**

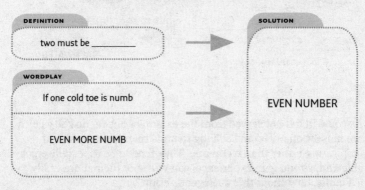

I have lost count of the number of times people have given me this as their favourite clue. It is a symbolic representation rather than a clue and evidently appeared many years ago.

NOVELTY CLUE: H I J K L M N O (5)

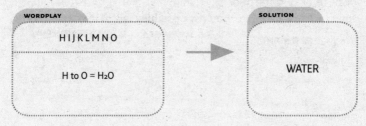

Its extension, listed next, might tickle your fancy:

NOVELTY CLUE: O N M L K J I H (9)

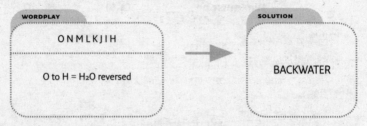

O N M L K J I H

O to H = H_2O reversed

→ BACKWATER

As you will have observed from the examples above, **novelty** clues are mostly 'one-offs' and solving them is therefore a matter of inspiration rather than technique. They tend to be especially enjoyable and, as you gain experience, you will spot them more easily.

Finally, how about this outrageous effort?

NOVELTY CLUE: OF, OF, OF, OF, OF, OF, OF, OF, OF, OF (10)

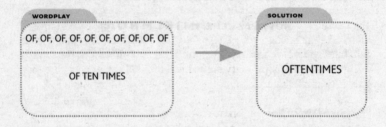

OF, OF, OF, OF, OF, OF, OF, OF, OF, OF

OF TEN TIMES

→ OFTENTIMES

9. Finer Points of Clues: General

> 'I attempted yesterday's Times crossword and managed to complete
> three clues – quid, Turgenev and courtier. I can only improve.'
> Lord Archer, A Prison Diary

Now to some points that are unrelated to specific clue types.

1. Complex constructions

Until now we have been concerned with demonstrating how to
solve clues that have one or two elements of trickery within them.
Most clues do follow this pattern but should you be daunted by
those which have even more? I'd say not at all: it's still a question
of decoding the separate elements, each of which will be signalled
in its own way. Even if the word defined is an unusual one and the
wordplay complex, you follow the indicators eventually to arrive at
the solution. The complex clue is reserved usually for intractable
words (as in the following *Times* clue), for which the setter can find
no alternative. Don't worry if you find this too unreasonably difficult (I do, too!) as simplicity is the ideal of most setters – a clue like
this is thankfully rare:

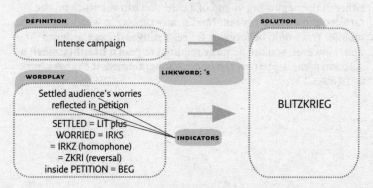

**COMPLEX CLUE – SANDWICH INCLUDING REVERSAL AND
HOMOPHONE: Intense campaign's settled audience's worries
reflected in petition (10)**

DEFINITION

Intense campaign

SOLUTION

WORDPLAY

Settled audience's worries
reflected in petition

SETTLED = LIT plus
WORRIED = IRKS
= IRKZ (homophone)
= ZKRI (reversal)
inside PETITION = BEG

LINKWORD: 's

INDICATORS

BLITZKRIEG

This next clue was also tough to solve as I discovered, not least because it is constructed with the somewhat artifical word *lower* (see Chapter 10). Also, it has no linking words and *Sgt Lewis* (he's gained promotion since) finds himself split into two between word-play and definition.

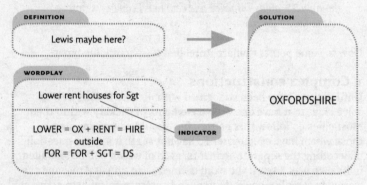

COMPLEX CLUE – SANDWICH: Lower rent houses for Sgt Lewis maybe here? (11)

DEFINITION

Lewis maybe here?

WORDPLAY

Lower rent houses for Sgt

LOWER = OX + RENT = HIRE
outside
FOR = FOR + SGT = DS

INDICATOR

SOLUTION

OXFORDSHIRE

Faced with either of the above two clues, I'd certainly defer any decoding until some intersecting help was available.

2. Definition placement

'I hate definitions.'
Benjamin Disraeli, *Vivian Gray*

As you know by now, the definition in clues is virtually always either at the beginning or end of a clue; you can get stuck on the rare occasion when it is not. Next is an example in which it is in the middle. You would be forgiven for regarding *instil* as the defini-tion. However, you are actually required to read it like this: when a solution meaning part of the body is anagrammed, it changes into *instil awe*.

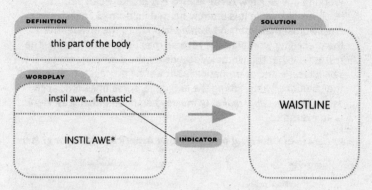

ANAGRAM CLUE: Instil awe when this part of the body is fantastic! (9)

DEFINITION
this part of the body

WORDPLAY
instil awe... fantastic!

INSTIL AWE*

INDICATOR

SOLUTION
WAISTLINE

3. Linkwords

Fairly commonly, the linkword has to be taken as one form in the surface reading and a different form in the cryptic reading. In this example, the use of 's means possessive pronoun in the former and is in the latter.

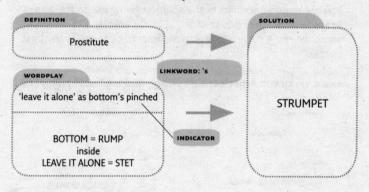

SANDWICH CLUE: Prostitute's 'leave it alone' as bottom's pinched (8)

DEFINITION
Prostitute

WORDPLAY
'leave it alone' as bottom's pinched

BOTTOM = RUMP
inside
LEAVE IT ALONE = STET

LINKWORD: 's

INDICATOR

SOLUTION
STRUMPET

TOP TIP – DIRECTION OF LINKWORDS

Working out which way the linkword is pointing can be tricky. For example, while it is entirely normal (in normal English and crosswords) that *from* and *leading to* point to the answer from the preceding wordplay, the reverse may occasionally apply. The test is whether the wordplay stands for the definition: that is to say, it clearly and grammatically shows the process which gives the solution. By stretching the language, some linkwords such as *get*, *gets*, *getting*, *makes* or *making* can point either way. Here is an example:

ANAGRAM CLUE: Fiscal policy making Americans go wrong? (11)

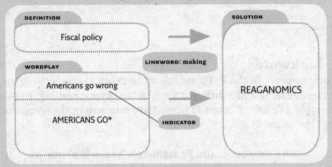

You are required to think of the solution giving rise to the **anagram fodder**. The reverse order, as in my reworked clue below, would be more natural and is more likely to be found in the best puzzles.

ANAGRAM CLUE: Americans go wrong making fiscal policy (11)

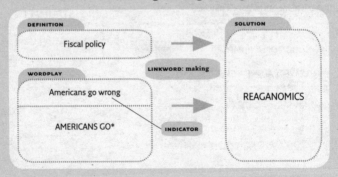

4. Punctuation: misleading

Apart from question marks and exclamation marks (see next paragraph), punctuation is by convention in all crosswords unreliable. This is especially confusing to beginners who have to be reminded that it may mislead and may have to be ignored. For example, the components of an anagram can be split across a full stop or a comma.

MISLEADING PUNCTUATION – ANAGRAM CLUE:
Exciting parcel, and she barely moves close (3,6)

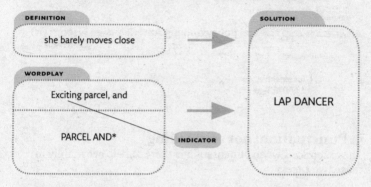

DEFINITION

she barely moves close

WORDPLAY

Exciting parcel, and

PARCEL AND*   INDICATOR

SOLUTION

LAP DANCER

Or punctuation can mislead by separating the parts to be initialized, i.e. first letters are to be taken from words either side of the comma, as seen here:

MISLEADING PUNCTUATION – ADDITIVE CLUE:
Diamonds are real, asked initially – sauce! (9)

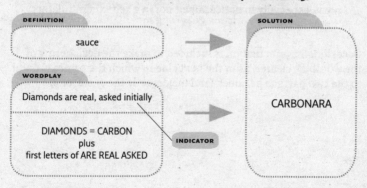

DEFINITION

sauce

WORDPLAY

Diamonds are real, asked initially

DIAMONDS = CARBON
plus
first letters of ARE REAL ASKED   INDICATOR

SOLUTION

CARBONARA

Punctuation can be omitted, too, as here where the comma required by the cryptic reading between the last two words (as in 'I, say') is not shown in the second definition:

MISLEADING PUNCTUATION – DOUBLE DEFINITION CLUE:
'Excellent', I say (7)

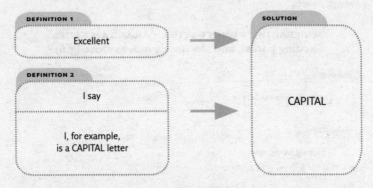

DEFINITION 1

Excellent

DEFINITION 2

I say

I, for example,
is a CAPITAL letter

SOLUTION

CAPITAL

5. Punctuation: not misleading

The exceptions when punctuation is there to help are mainly in these two cases:

- **Question mark**: as a hint that the solution either is slightly tenuous, or it's an example of a group rather than a synonym. Thus *apple* to define *fruit* may well have a question mark.
- **Exclamation mark**: as an indication either that something most unusual is going on within the clue, or that the clue has a remarkable or humorous feature that the setter wants you especially to notice, albeit not in a self-congratulatory manner.

Occasionally, punctuation is included to make the deciphering of the wordplay clearer, as in the next clue in which the commas point to the two parts to be added (and incidentally the *of* = *o'* or *o*).

HELPFUL PUNCTUATION – ADDITIVE CLUE INCLUDING SANDWICH: It's put on bow of ship, initially, one in the navy (5)

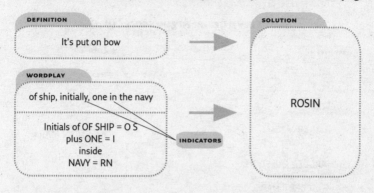

DEFINITION

It's put on bow

WORDPLAY

of ship, initially, one in the navy

Initials of OF SHIP = O S
plus ONE = I
inside
NAVY = RN

INDICATORS

SOLUTION

ROSIN

TOP TIP – WHAT DO ELLIPSES IN CLUES MEAN?

The answer is simple: it's merely a way of connecting two clues (sometimes more) to present a longer than normal clue sentence, i.e. across the two clues. Each clue stands on its own with regard to definition and wordplay (even if one part references another). Here is an example in which the first is an **additive** and the second a **double definition**:

TWO CLUES LINKED BY ELLIPSES:
5 down: Annoyed on account of one bird... (9)
6 down: ...fleeces others (5)

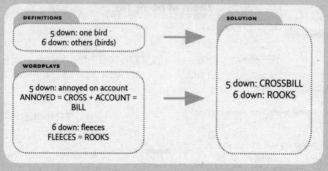

DEFINITIONS

5 down: one bird
6 down: others (birds)

WORDPLAYS

5 down: annoyed on account
ANNOYED = CROSS + ACCOUNT = BILL

6 down: fleeces
FLEECES = ROOKS

SOLUTION

5 down: CROSSBILL
6 down: ROOKS

Finally, here is an example of punctuation not only being helpful but forming the definition:

ADDITIVE CLUE: Argue score? (8,4)

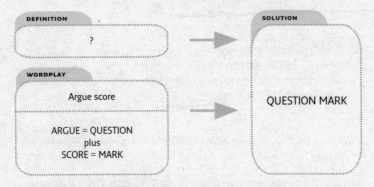

DEFINITION

?

SOLUTION

WORDPLAY

Argue score

QUESTION MARK

ARGUE = QUESTION
plus
SCORE = MARK

I would not be surprised if you are somewhat discombobulated by the points in the above section. They are undoubtedly tricky but I'm sure you will eventually find punctuation no major problem.

6. More deceptive linkwords

In section 3 of this chapter we saw one deceptive use of the 's. The clue below shows another. The apostrophe looks at first glance as though it may be a **linkword** (for *is*) but in fact it's an adjectival synonym for the solution.

SANDWICH CLUE: Woman's very good protecting them at home (8)

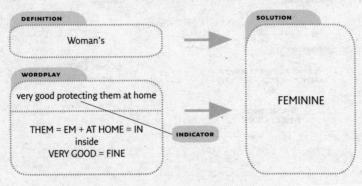

DEFINITION

Woman's

SOLUTION

WORDPLAY

very good protecting them at home

INDICATOR

FEMININE

THEM = EM + AT HOME = IN
inside
VERY GOOD = FINE

7. Crossword war horses

There are inevitably some crossword terms that occur time and again, often words of two, three or four letter words. It is impossible to list all of them here but those in this P. G. Wodehouse quotation (from *Meet Mr Mulliner*) may still be seen today:

> *'George spent his evenings doing the crossword puzzle. By the time he was thirty he knew more about Eli, the prophet, Ra the Sun God and the bird Emu than anybody else in the country except the vicar's daughter who had also taken up the solving of crossword puzzles and was the first girl in Worcestershire to find out the meaning of stearine and crepuscular.'*

A military war horse is an American Civil War General who is still honoured in crosswords, as in this next clue. It seems that solvers are required never to forget those whose names are frequently thrown up by normal English words such as in the answer below:

SANDWICH CLUE: General secures unit some drink (8)

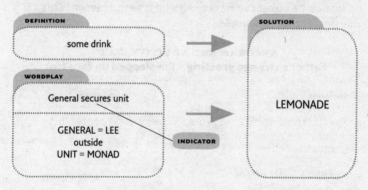

DEFINITION

some drink

SOLUTION

WORDPLAY

General secures unit

GENERAL = LEE
outside
UNIT = MONAD

INDICATOR

LEMONADE

8. Stuttering clues

A sentence uttered stutteringly is indicated by repetition, as follows:

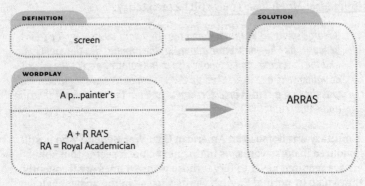

ADDITIVE CLUE: A p...painter's screen (5)

DEFINITION		SOLUTION
screen	→	

WORDPLAY		
A p...painter's	→	ARRAS
A + R RA'S RA = Royal Academician		

9. Use of first person singular

An inanimate object can be defined as if it were a person. This amusing clue is an example:

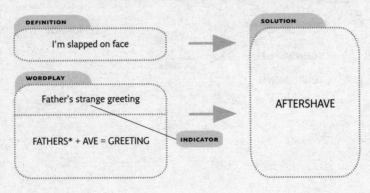

ANAGRAM AND ADDITIVE CLUE:
Father's strange greeting – I'm slapped on face (10)

DEFINITION		SOLUTION
I'm slapped on face	→	

WORDPLAY		
Father's strange greeting	→	AFTERSHAVE
FATHERS* + AVE = GREETING	INDICATOR	

10. Real people

Some newspapers are cautious with regard to clues referring to or defining real people. They are happy with this beauty about former VIPs:

SANDWICH CLUE: Love's admitted by His Majesty King Edward, becoming Mrs Simpson's husband (5)

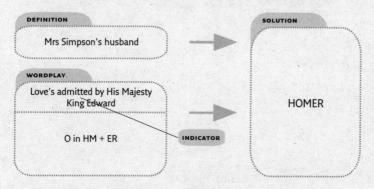

DEFINITION		SOLUTION
Mrs Simpson's husband	→	
WORDPLAY		HOMER
Love's admitted by His Majesty King Edward	→	
O in HM + ER	INDICATOR	

The trend though, notably in the *Guardian* and the *Independent*, is to revel in clues such as this one about a living person:

HOMOPHONE CLUE: Smear former Labour leader in Liverpool? (4)

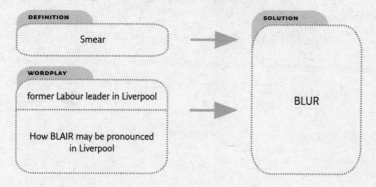

DEFINITION		SOLUTION
Smear	→	
WORDPLAY		BLUR
former Labour leader in Liverpool	→	
How BLAIR may be pronounced in Liverpool		

10. Ten Especially Troublesome Words

'My agent rings, she says: "I'm stuck on the crossword. The clue's 'Overloaded postman'." I pause a moment: "How many letters?" "Hundreds."'

Jeremy Paxman, *Spectator* diary

Either because they have multiple uses, or because they are a well-established convention but not immediately obvious, there are a few particularly awkward words which it's good to know about. The first two, *about* and *in*, are especially difficult for newcomers.

1. About

One of the most misleading words in crosswords is *about* because it has so many uses:

- a **reversal** indicator of whole words, or parts of them, in across and down clues
- a **sandwich** indicator
- an **anagram** indicator
- *C*, *CA* as abbreviations
- a synonym for *re* and *on*

2. In

Likewise the innocent little multi-purpose word *in* causes trouble. Each of these next clues uses *in* differently. First, as a **hidden** indicator:

HIDDEN CLUE: In Amritsar, it's a common habit (4)

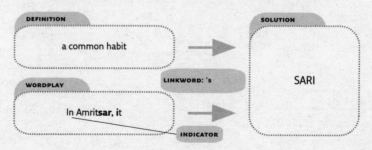

DEFINITION
a common habit

SOLUTION
SARI

WORDPLAY
In Amrit**sar, it**

LINKWORD: 's

INDICATOR

Second, as a **linkword** between definition and wordplay:

ADDITIVE CLUE: **Be prolific in area before spring (6)**

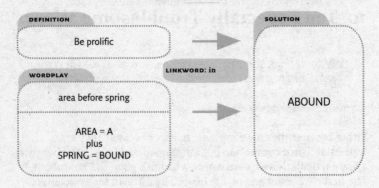

Third, as a **sandwich** indicator:

SANDWICH CLUE: **Clearly aren't in use (10)**

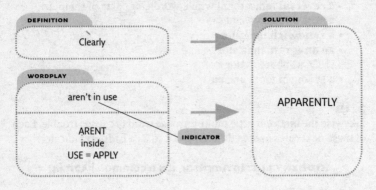

Fourth (though rarely), as a **definition**:

SANDWICH CLUE: In goal, blocking attempt (6)

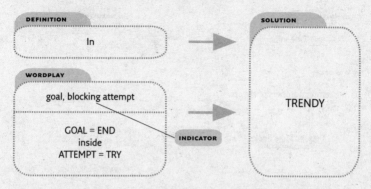

DEFINITION
In

WORDPLAY
goal, blocking attempt

GOAL = END
inside
ATTEMPT = TRY

INDICATOR

SOLUTION
TRENDY

Fifth (equally rarely), as a **definition** in another language:

CRYPTIC DEFINITION: This is in French (2,7)

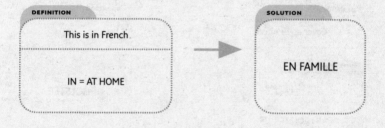

DEFINITION
This is in French.

IN = AT HOME

SOLUTION
EN FAMILLE

Sixth, as part of the **definition**:

HOMOPHONE CLUE: One in bed reciting numbers of sheep (5)

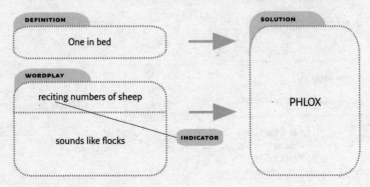

DEFINITION
One in bed → **SOLUTION**

WORDPLAY
reciting numbers of sheep

sounds like flocks → **INDICATOR**

PHLOX

Seventh, as part of the **wordplay**:

ADDITIVE CLUE: Cover up furniture in court case (9)

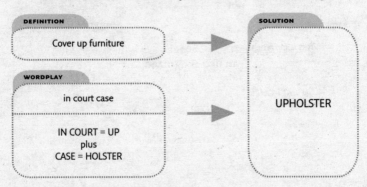

DEFINITION
Cover up furniture → **SOLUTION**

WORDPLAY
in court case

IN COURT = UP
plus
CASE = HOLSTER

UPHOLSTER

The first, second and third of these usages are by far the most common.

3. Without

This can be an indication that something must be taken away, as below:

TAKEAWAY CLUE: Drink that's sweet, without ice (6)

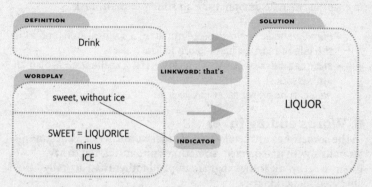

In some puzzles, *without* is also still used in the sense of *outside* (marked as archaic in most dictionaries). It is therefore a **sandwich** indicator, as follows:

SANDWICH CLUE: Gardens without nitrogen can be recognized (4)

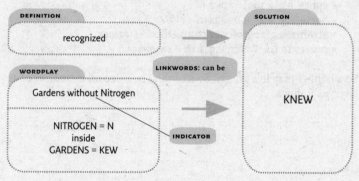

4. One

The word *one* can be a **wordplay** substitute for *I, ace, a, an* and *un* (from the dialect usage *'un*).

5. Men

In cryptics, men do demonstrate an ability to multi-task:

- *man* can be *he*, a chess piece or pawn, a soldier, an island as in the Isle of Man, or just a plain fellow
- *male* can be *m* or *he* (which as HE – His Excellency – is also an ambassador)
- *men* can be *or* (for *other ranks*)

6. Words ending in -er

In the sometimes artificial world of crosswords, we can encounter nouns with unexpected, sometimes unnatural, not to say groan-worthy, meanings that are implied rather than actually specified in dictionaries.

Here are some which can serve to indicate anything that:

- flows, e.g. a river or stream – *flower*
- blooms, e.g. a flower – *bloomer*
- numbs, e.g. an anaesthetic or an anaesthetist – *number*
- lows, e.g. a cow, an ox – *lower*
- splits, e.g. a tool – *river*
- butts, e.g. a goat or a ram – *butter*
- strains, e.g. tug-of-war competitor – *strainer*
- moves in the water, e.g. fish – *swimmer*

So a banker may live in, say, Switzerland but also on the banks of a river, as follows:

ADDITIVE (DOWN) CLUE INCLUDING REVERSAL:
Love to upset an African banker (5)

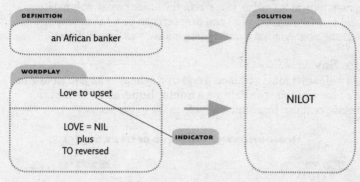

7. Of

Of can very occasionally be a linking word between the solution and wordplay. Its meaning in this case is stretched (arguably too far) to *from* or *constituted by* as here in this example:

SANDWICH (DOWN) CLUE INCLUDING REVERSAL:
Prehistoric city's taken up in an issue of learning (9)

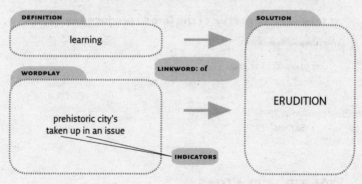

8 & 9. Right and left

Right and *left* appear in a number of guises. *Right* can be an **anagram** indicator (= verb, *to correct*); the letter *r* as an abbreviation; and synonyms such as *ok* and *lien*. *Left* can be a **takeaway** indicator; the abbreviation *l*; and synonyms such as *over* and *port*.

10. Say

As well as its most common usage as a synonym for *for example* or *e.g.*, the word *say* can indicate a **homophone**, as in the first clue below, or it can be a simple synonym, as in the second:

HOMOPHONE CLUE: Shrub or trees, say (5)

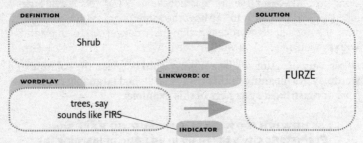

ALL-IN-ONE ADDITIVE CLUE: One to produce key, say (6)

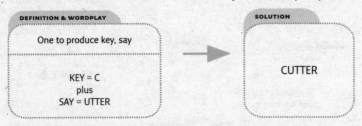

TOP TIP – KEY NOTES
The word *key* (as in the previous clue) and its sister, *note*, can have a lot of forms in their various musical guises. As regards phonetic notes, they are these: *do, doh, re, mi, me, fa, so, soh, la, lah, te, ti*; or they can be single letters: *a, b, c, d, e, f, g*. Despite this unwanted luxury of choice, you should normally find clues with any of these references leave you in no doubt which note is required.

11: A Solving Sequence

'I wish he would explain his explanation.'
Lord Byron, Don Juan

In this chapter I take a cryptic from the *Independent* and record my solving process. Of course, mine is not the only way to success but I hope you find it helpful to see how the mind of at least one solver works. It's not a speedy process as I'm more concerned to enjoy and savour the journey; if you want to see how the mind of a champion speed solver works, do try the blog referred to at the foot of page 141.

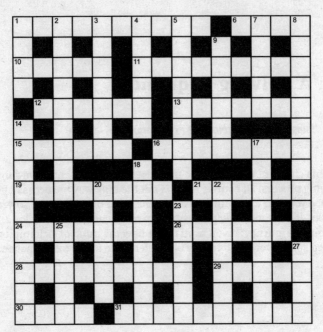

Across

1 Picture of Ford's early form of transport (10)
6 Course in homeopathy (4)
10 A chapter penned by him rejected for book (5)
11 Pro tense about Wimbledon final – for so long? (9)
12 Story-teller's book, in brief prepared for distribution (6)
13 Greek ambassador accepts measure, heralding new start for economy (7)
15 Suit Scottish team (6)
16 Begs food after rent's settled (8)
19 Thespian overcome with embarrassment? One needs to make some changes (8)
21 Act with energy? Not if this (6)
24 Two fighters stuck in drifting E-boat? That's odd (7)
26 A head chef regularly presented a pastry dish for starters (6)
28 Recidivist prisoner on trial? Outcome's already known (2,7)
29 It could take truck to heart of Europe (5)
30 Story's thread (4)
31 Broadcast reporting about old movement's founder (10)

Down

1 Languages used in Assam, India (4)
2 Companion entertained by a bawdy chap (9)
3 Old horse, one with curb attached for parade (7)
4 Steer onto ring road, bypassing entrance to French city (6)
5 Hands-free mobile? Hard to find fault initially, with one (3,5)
7 Rolling Stones song - big hit but not top, that is (5)
8 Woman's wise to go beyond Derby, say, for Peak District village (10)
9 Fisherman shows annoyance, getting line caught (6)
14 White wine acceptable with green vegetable? No (10)
17 Battle opposing start of Communism, before our time (9)
18 American sports fan clutches empty bottle, wanting drink (4,4)
20 Valets maybe requiring energy when employed by families (6)
22 Awfully moronic letter from 13 (7)
23 Tabloid's name for hoi polloi (6)
25 Difficulty, one admitted by father (5)
27 Mock monarch's self-introduction in Franglais? (4)

More often than not, my starting point is a long **anagram**, found via an indicator. That's of course because lots of intersecting letters are useful. Here there are none such, so Plan B: go for a **hidden**, usually yielding smaller words. I'm in luck today as this one occurs early on in a routine scan of across clues:

6 A: Course in homeopathy (4)
This is short enough to be a double definition but it's a **hidden** clue with the *course* being *path*. I know that many people find hidden letters more or less straightaway, but I also know that many do not. As I said earlier, a crossword workshop group typically splits about equally on this. Luckily I'm in the first category so we are on the right *path* fairly early.

First letters are valuable so let's try the *a* from *path* in...

7 D: Rolling Stones song – big hit but not top, that is (5)
Not being a rock fan, the answer does not come to mind, even after spotting *that is* being i.e., thereby making *a--ie Annie*? No, can't be as the remaining three letters have to be a *hit* without the first letter and in any case I can't imagine Mick Jagger doing that soppy musical.

On to the H, an encouraging first letter:

8 D: Woman's wise to go beyond Derby, say, for Peak District village (10)
Woman's must be *her*, *wise* is almost always *sage* so we have ---*hersage*. Don't recognise anything yet until the *say* after *Derby* makes me think of headgear.

Look up *Hathersage* and there it is in reliable Wikipedia. Good for a small village to be so honoured and good that the setter has given us a suitably friendly clue. Maybe it's close to his home.

A brief look at 11 Across gets nowhere but the eye catches *ambassador* in 13 across and that must be *he*:

13 A: Greek ambassador accepts measure, heralding new start for economy (7)
The definition is more likely to be *Greek* at the front of the clue than *economy* at the end. *Accepts* shows a **sandwich** so *he----e* (more likely than *h----ee*) enables a guess at *Hellene*. Working back (most important in avoiding false entries which delay you inordinately) it's *ell* as the measure added to *n* for *new* plus *e(conomy)*.

I spot *line* in 9 down, viz:

9 D: Fisherman shows annoyance, getting line caught (6)

That could be the *l* we have from *Hellene*. *Line* is most appropriate as *Fisherman* is involved. Try *angler* with *annoyance* being *anger*. A **sandwich** again.

The grid now looks like this:

11 across doesn't get us far so let's go to 21 across to exploit the *g* final letter. The obvious is an *-ing* word so try to relate that to the clue:

21 A: Act with energy? Not if this (6)

Doesn't have an *-ing* in it so maybe it's something else. An **additive** clue, probably, with the last three words as the **definition**. Is the cunning setter trying to mislead us into thinking *energy* is *e* (which it usually is)? Possibly but this time we know better as *zing* fits and *act* can be *do*. Put them together and we insert *dozing*. Not as hard as it looked.

That gives an *o* as first of 22 down:

22 D: Awfully moronic letter from 13 (7)

The **anagram** indicator *awfully* rings bells and the 13 refers to *Hellene* so unscrambling the **anagram fodder** *moronic* quickly brings on the Greek letter *omicron*. As an aside, I'm not keen on cross referenced clues, especially when there are lots of them, but here it's no problem.

A five-letter word starting with *r* is enticing and here it is:

29 A: It could take truck to heart of Europe (5)

Heart of Europe is *ro* so in an **additive** clue, a three-letter van is required. Even then, what's the definition? Well, it must be an **all-in-one** clue and *route* would be one answer. What's *ute* then? Ah! I remember now: it's a pick-up truck down under (presumably short for 'utility truck').

Now to 16 across but nothing seems to fit that. Quickly then, following the intersecting letters, go to 17 down:

17 D: Battle opposing start of Communism, before our time (9)

Finding the definition is half the battle and here it's the whole *battle* as it's unlikely that the last 1, 2 or 3 words will provide a definition. *Opposing* can be *agin* and *Agincourt* is the answer. Still safer to confirm via wordplay which is *c* plus *our* and *t* for *time*.

To 26 across (*--i-c-*) next:

26 A: A head chef regularly presented a pastry dish for starters (6)

You see *regularly* regularly in cryptics. It means: take the alternate letters usually and that gives *hf* or *ce* from *chef*. Must be the latter, slotting into the *--i-c-* as the final two letters. *A pie* might feature so add that to make *apiece*. That reflects a highly misleading definition, *a head* in the sense of *for each person*. Wow! Brilliant, albeit tough clue about food that prompts me to get up to pour a glass of Chardonnay.

Now refreshed, I go to 23 down leading nowhere but 31 across looks promising with *broadcast*:

31 A: Broadcast reporting about old movement's founder (10)

In its meaning of 'spread about', that indicates an anagram and the *o* for *old* gives the necessary ten letters. Take *about* as being a sandwich indicator (there are other uses made of that tricky word – see page 101) and you get *o* inside anagram of *reporting* for *progenitor*, the *founder* in question.

That gives a *g* as last letter in 23 down so how about another *...ing*? A glance at the clue:

23 D: Tabloid's name for hoi polloi (6)

This doesn't give much to support that, but *tabloid* is a *rag* in crossword terms even if the *Independent* wouldn't agree. Something *rag* then? No, so go elsewhere.

27 D: Mock monarch's self-introduction in Franglais? (4)

-e-r is *leer, beer, seer*? Try *jeer* which contains *je* to explain the Franglais *self-introduction*. With the *monarch* being *er* we've justified a cheeky novelty-type clue. Not to be jeered at, for sure!

Still seeking signs of anagrams, *settled* looks a candidate. That's in:

16 A: Begs food after rent's settled (8)

Considering the *s* as final letter (but not putting it in yet), *begs* would be the definition. Mix *rent* into *entr*, add *eats* for *food* and we have *entreats*.

On to *-h-n-* as the second word in a (3,5) in:

5 D: Hands-free mobile? Hard to find fault initially, with one (3,5)

With *mobile* in the clue, *phone* it has to be. *Find fault* gives *carp* and a High Street warehouse (*Car Phone*)has the right ring about it.

11 and 1 across both prove fruitless so let's have another shot at 23 down:

23 D: Tabloid's name for hoi polloi (6)

Funny how returning to a half-solved clue is easier second time. It's *ragtag* with *name* being *tag*.

The grid is now:

28 across has *trial* in a nine-letter answer so *test* probably has a part to play.

28 A: Recidivist prisoner on trial? Outcome's already known (2,7)

Interesting how many times parts of answers are helping and here's another: *prisoner* is *con* so often that it is worth a shot. *Recidivist* is an unusual indication of a reversal (but why not?) and *no contest* is the entry.

The central *c* in 25 down could be from *ace* (equals *one* which has so many possibilities – see page 106) and so it proves. Mastering the three- and four-letter words is a significant part of success and probably helps to explain how seasoned solvers are successful.

25 D: Difficulty, one admitted by father (5)

With *father* = *fr* forming the outside of the sandwich, *facer* goes in though not before a quick dictionary check.

Abbreviations are also a means to an end and *fighters* being *f* (as in F-16 et al) signifies *ff* in the build-up to the next customer:

24 A: Two fighters stuck in drifting E-boat? That's odd (7)
Drifting is probably an anagram indicator and the five letters
of *eboat* give us the needed seven total. *Odd* is *offbeat* so that's
inserted.

I find double definitions are often best left till last but may be
worth a quick guess. That pays off here in:

30 A: Story's thread (4)
as *--r-* gives *yarn*. I imagine many would find that came quickly.

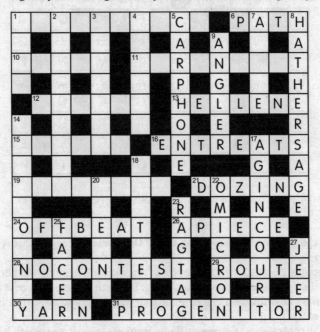

So much intersecting help is now available in 14 down :

14 D: White wine acceptable with green vegetable? No (10)
with *o-n-y* as the bottom five and the definition probably *white* or
white wine. *No* at the other end of the clue is odd but all becomes
clear as *Chardonnay* pops up. Just finished my glass thereof so time
for another. The *vegetable* is *chard* plus *on* and *nay* for *no* completes
the story, though I disagree with its sentiment on the accompani-
ment for vegetables. Surface readings can't be entirely accurate for
everyone.

Anyway, that's a real step forward as two initial letters are available. Let's go with the *h*:

15 A: Suit Scottish team (6)

There are many multi-meaning terms in card games and *suit* is one. As I'm more of a soccer than a rock fan, *hearts* comes to mind.

The next initial letter is *r* in this one:

19 A: Thespian overcome with embarrassment? One needs to make some changes (8)

Must be *red* something but what? *Thespian* for *actor* and now we have it (*redactor*) – the actor must have fluffed his lines.

Next to 20 down with *c-e-n-* and this clue:

20 D: Valets maybe requiring energy when employed by families (6)

It's often a good thing to switch parts of speech and the noun *valet* is also a verb. Also here is *e* for *energy* in its normal guise, put inside *clans* for *families* to give *cleans*.

That leaves the 18 down clue with some letters:

18 D: American sports fan clutches empty bottle, wanting drink (4,4)

Empty bottle gives *be* (nothing inside it, not like my glass) and *root* would fit the *beer*? Check *rooter* and it is an American fan.

2 and 3 down have last letters available to build on but *d* and *t* are not enough. So a complete change now, as we go into the dark with no letters to help.

OK, keep calm, have another swig and look for anagrams. We've only had one so far; surely one or two remain? No luck apparently but *used in* at 1 down could reveal a hidden clue:

1 D: Languages used in Assam, India (4)

Not the Pakistani cricketer *Sami* but a Lappish word. Living for some years in Finland where it's a common name, helped a lot there. So the *s* and *c* in 1 across might get us that important one:

1 A: Picture of Ford's early form of transport (10)

Enjoy thinking of the Model T (a frequent form of transport in crosswords) and think of other *ford*s, especially one related to *pic-ture*s. Ah ha as Alan Partridge says, it must be John F and the movie *Stagecoach*.

Sticking with first letters, *m* in 10 across is next for our decoding:

10 A: A chapter penned by him rejected for book (5)

Reverse *him*, put it outside *a c* (for *a chapter*) also reversed, relate it to *book* and we have *Micah*. Note that the whole lot has to be reversed, not just the *him*, as one might have first thought.

The *o* of 4 down is promising:

4 D: Steer onto ring road, bypassing entrance to French city (6)

French city beginning with *o*? I only know *Orleans* and that's seven letters. *Bypassing* indicates a sandwich that would include the *f* from *French*. Hence *city* is the definition and it's not a *French city* at all. Perhaps it's *Oxford*? Well *steer* can be *ox* and *ring road* can be *o rd*. Put it in. Now let's turn to *f-r-n---t*, guessable as *fortnight* but why?

11 A: Pro tense about Wimbledon final – for so long? (9)

Well, it is *for* = *pro*, *tense* = *tight* with *n* taken in to make *fortnight*. A lot of sandwiches in this puzzle, but no complaints as they are all fairly indicated and they give me an excuse to glug a drop of wine again.

The grid now is nearly filled:

Back to the *stones* in 7 down:

7 D: Rolling Stones song – big hit but not top, that is (5)

Check on *Angie* and find it was a 1973 single. Good old Wiki coming to the rescue again.

What about *e-h* ending in *t* in 3 down?

3 D: Old horse, one with curb attached for parade (7)

Exhaunt, *exhaust* or *exhibit*? *Parade* confirms the latter. An additive clue this time with *ex h i* and *bit* for *curb* unpacking it.

Not sure why I didn't notice *story-teller* in the clue below earlier, especially as it has an anagram indicator:

12 A: Story-teller's book, in brief prepared for distribution (6)

Yes, *prepared for distribution*, three words telling the solver to mix *brief* around *b* for *book* for *fibber*. Very nicely devious as *brief* is used more often as 'deduct the last letter'. Not sure why but Chambers shows the clothing usage as *short in length* so that's fine.

Only one more:

2 D: Companion entertained by a bawdy chap (9)
The last (13th) sandwich clue signalled by *entertained* and a minimal
definition of *chap*. But if you know that *companion* is *ch* (of Honour),
Archibald comes to mind. *A ribald* outside is the last piece of the
jigsaw.

So that's the final grid. A most enjoyable solve benefiting from
absolute fairness in the wordplay and many misleading words. Only
one complete anagram and four partial ones is fewer than for other
puzzles in this book and this arguably makes for a slightly longer
solving experience but we shouldn't mind. We've enjoyed a leisurely
stroll whilst appreciating the joys of the English language (and
lovely French wine).

The setter was DAC, a regular in the *Independent* and thanks to
him for the entertainment.

Here are the explanations, summarised. **Definitions** are in bold,
indicators are <u>underlined</u>.

Clue type	What you have to do	Solution
Across		
1 Picture of Ford's early form of transport		
double def.	Think movies	Stagecoach
6 Course in homeopathy		
hidden	Look inside homeopathy	path
10 A chapter penned by him rejected for **book**		
sandwich incl. reversal	Put a c inside him all reversed	Micah
11 Pro tense about Wimbledon final – for **so long**?		
sandwich	Put n inside for tight	fortnight
12 Story-teller's book, in brief prepared for distribution		
sandwich incl. anagram	Put b inside anagram brief	fibber
13 Greek ambassador accepts measure, heralding new start for economy		
additive incl. sandwich	Put ell inside he, add n e	Hellene
15 Suit Scottish team		
double def.	Think cards	hearts
16 Begs food after rent's settled		
additive incl. anagram	Add anagram rent to eats	entreats
19 Thespian overcome with embarrassment? **One needs to make some changes**		
additive	Think red actor	redactor
21 Act with energy? Not if this		
additive	Add do to zing	dozing
24 Two fighters stuck in drifting E-boat? That's **odd**		
sandwich incl. anagram	Put ff inside anagram eboat	offbeat

26 **A head** chef <u>regularly</u> presented a pastry dish for starters

additive *incl. takeaway*	Add *a pie* to *c(h)e(f)*	apiece

28 <u>Recidivist</u> prisoner on trial? **Outcome's already known**

additive *incl. reversal*	Reverse *con*, add to *on test*	no contest

29 **It could take truck to heart of Europe**

all-in-one *additive*	Add *ute* = truck to *(eu)ro(pe)*	route

30 **Story's thread**

double def.	Think type of	yarn

31 <u>Broadcast</u> reporting <u>about</u> old **movement's founder**

sandwich *incl. anagram*	Put *o* inside anagram *reporting*	progenitor

Down

1 **Languages** <u>used in</u> Assam, India

hidden	Look inside *Assam India*	Sami

2 Companion <u>entertained</u> by a bawdy **chap**

sandwich	Put *ch* inside *a ribald*	Archibald

3 Old horse, one with curb attached for **parade**

additive	Add *exh i bit*	exhibit

4 Steer onto ring road, <u>bypassing</u> entrance to French **city**

sandwich	Put F inside *ox o rd*	Oxford

5 **Hands-free mobile?** Hard to find fault initially, with one

additive	Add *carp* to *h one*	car phone

7 **Rolling Stones song** – big hit <u>but not top</u>, that is

takeaway	Add *(b)ang* to *ie*	Angie

8 Woman's wise to go beyond Derby, say, for **Peak District village**

additive	Add *hat* to *her sage*	Hathersage

9 **Fisherman** shows annoyance, getting line <u>caught</u>

sandwich	Put *l* inside *anger*	angler

14 **White wine** acceptable with green vegetable? No

additive	Add *chard on nay*	Chardonnay

17 **Battle** opposing start of Communism, before our time

additive	Add *agin* to *c our t*	Agincourt

18 American sports fan <u>clutches</u> empty bottle, wanting **drink**

sandwich	Put *b(ottl)e* inside *rooter*	root beer

20 **Valets** maybe requiring energy when <u>employed by</u> families

sandwich	Put *e* inside *clans*	cleans

22 <u>Awfully</u> moronic **letter from 13**

anagram	Mix *moronic*	omicron

23 Tabloid's name for **hoi polloi**

additive	Add *rag* to *tag*	ragtag

25 **Difficulty** one admitted by father

sandwich	Put *ace* inside *fr*	facer

27 **Mock monarch's self-introduction in Franglais?**

novelty	Think I in French	jeer

12: Ten Ways to Raise Your Game

'Reporters observed Mrs Attlee's eccentric driving as the Prime Minister busied himself with crosswords in the back of his car.'
Kevin Jeffrey, *Finest and Darkest Hours*

We will now look at methods that you might consider for improving your crossword-solving skills.

1. Practice, practice, practice!
This is the number one recommendation for improvement. There are many verbal tricks and conventions that are more easily recognized after you have done lots of crosswords. That still leaves room for setters to provide new ones, so have no fear that boredom will set in! You may like to practise by trying some of the clues and puzzles later in the book.

2. Solve with a friend
People often tell me that they enjoy doing all or part of the puzzle with a family member or work colleague. This can be face-to-face or by the many electronic ways available but whichever is used, there seems to be a significant solving improvement. Incidentally, after one of my workshops, the participants formed an internet-based group to help each other solve their daily crossword.

3. Join an Online Crossword Club
Some of those available are run by the *Daily Mail*, *Daily Express*, *Daily Telegraph* and *The Times*. There is also a flourising Australian Crossword Club.

Whilst some of these are free, some require a relatively small payment and they supply a variety of attractions, several including Sudoku and other word-related puzzles. Most have archived puzzles which can be used for practice.

4. Join a terrestrial Crossword Club

This is the Crossword Club, based at Awbridge, Hampshire: contact details are on *www.thecrosswordclub.co.uk*.

For the past thirty five years, this club run by Brian Head has published a monthly magazine (both printed and electronic versions) with puzzles, articles and competitions. It also offers an agony aunt (the Cluru) for clue solution explanations that have defeated you.

5. Buy a book of crosswords

If good old-fashioned books are what you prefer, then one of the large number available may appeal. There are books for many of the puzzles mentioned in this book. Some discipline is of course needed as the solutions in the back are all too readily accessible before completion. An e-book purchase is an equally good idea, especially one with the ability to write in answers on an iPad. In this connection I'd recommend going to *www.puzzazz.com* as it links to a couple of books by Brian Greer (Brendan and Virgilius), three of whose crosswords and a good few example clues enhance this book.

6. Enjoy a fun crossword workshop

Strictly non-competitive, open to all of any age and whatever existing skills, a crossword workshop is a way to improve skills and experience. Details of those coming up in your area are available on various websites, including the author's at *www.timmoorey.info*. The first of these has run at Marlborough College in Wiltshire for the past 8 years and takes place on weekday mornings in late July.

Residential
Marlborough: www.mcsummerschool.org.uk
Somerset: www.dillington.com
Cotswolds: www.farncombeestate.co.uk

Non-residential
London: www.howtoacademy.com
Gloucestershire: www.thecoach-house.com

7. Try the Monday Crossword

Solvers of the *Daily Telegraph* and the *Guardian* cryptic consider that the first of the week is often easier than those for the rest of the week.

WHAT DISTINGUISHES THE LIBERTARIAN SCHOOL FROM THE XIMENEAN ONE?

It would take a lot of space to comment on this and I suspect many readers would not want to stay with me. A few examples will suffice. Libertarian clues may require the solver to split words like *indeed* into *in* and *deed* where, say, *part* is to be inserted to make the answer *departed*. You may also be required to stretch normal word meanings, as in an imaginative definition of composer Vivaldi. He has been clued as a 'seasonal barman'. This seems slightly degrading for the Red Priest but amusing nonetheless. Wagner has been similarly clued in a single word without further wordplay as 'Ringmaster (6)'.

Slight stretching of homophones for comic effect will be found. For example:
To make cheese, how do you milk a Welsh hedgehog? (10)
Answer: Caerphilly

Hidden clues may have superfluous words and disregard reality:
Most Richard Tauber records contain this bird (7)
Answer: ostrich

Single word clues may need splitting as here:
Ascribe? (8,5)
Answer: articled clerk

Indicators may be missing as is the reversal needed here:
Announcement to put into a French resort ((6)
Answer: notice

Rules of grammar are usually obeyed but not always:
A nut go into this (6)
Answer: nougat
To make it worse for Ximeneans, this clue also lacks a proper anagram indicator according to the precepts explained earlier.

Where would you find this type of clueing? Principally from some but by no means all setters in the *Guardian* where all the above clues appeared. However *Guardian* readers know what to expect and clearly greatly enjoy this *Anything Goes* school of clue-writing. They may well agree with the sentiment expressed by one solver to me that crosswords need to develop and should not be bound by a stickler classics master of over 50 years ago.

8. Study the published solutions

Though explanations are not published, it can be highly productive to study the solutions published and to work backwards for any clues you have not managed to crack. I believe many would like to see annotated solutions but space limitations prevail.

9. Study the blogs

These are covered in Chapter 13.

10. Study the website www.andlit.com

Maintained by John Tozer, this site is a treasure trove of prize-winning clues from the *Observer*'s Azed competition which began in 1972. Whilst the Azed crossword is of the barred type not covered here, hundreds of clues should make for a stimulating read and the commentary by Azed in his 'slip' could give a further insight into Ximenean principles.

PART 3

PRACTICE TIME

13: Ten Media Recommendations

'Unlike crossword fanatics I do actually read the paper.'
Bernice Rubens

There's much more help available than just a dictionary these days. In fact an increasing number of books, websites and electronic gadgets offer assistance as well as crosswords. Here are some recommendations:

1. Dictionaries

The principal dictionaries used by setters today for blocked cross-words are *Collins English Dictionary*, the *Concise Oxford Dictionary* and *Chambers*, the dictionary par excellence for barred crosswords. If the meaning of a word is in none of these, the most likely explanation is that it is a new usage. Note that Collins has reinstated names of people (*Beethoven* is now there as well as *Bonn*).

2. Thesauruses

Collins, Oxford and Chambers all publish useful dictionaries of synonyms and all three are more efficient for crossword solvers than the longer established *Roget's Thesaurus*, the use of which can involve lots of page-turning for any one reference.

3. Word list books:

***Collins Bradford's Crossword Solver's Dictionary*, 9th edition 2013:**
This has been the book of choice among the crossword public for twenty-five years, principally because of its method of production. Not having been compiled from computerized lists, it was, and continues to be, built up by its author, Anne Bradford, from solutions actually appearing in a variety of crosswords. That means you have a good chance of finding the name of, say, that elusive horse (well over 200 entries) to complete the puzzle.

Chambers Crossword Dictionary, 3rd edition, 2012:

This nicely complements *Bradford's*, as well as containing extra features, e.g. articles on crossword English, indicators and what constitutes a good clue. It is rare for an answer word in a daily not to be found in either of these two books, both of which are published in cheaper, pocket-sized editions.

4. Electronic aids

Pocket machines:

Sharp PWE300 or 500A

This includes the *Oxford Dictionary*, the *Oxford Thesaurus* and, in the case of the PWE500A, the *Oxford Dictionary of Quotations*, all searchable by individual words and phrases. Like the pocket machine recommended next, it has anagram and word search facilities. Thus, if you need to find a four- letter word ending in j you will do so easily and quickly. I have used the PWE500 (now PWE500A) for several years instead of carrying dictionaries and wordlist books around. However smartphone users can now access most of this and similar material easily and cheaply (see next section), perhaps accounting for the poor availability of this machine currently.

Bradford's Crossword Solver CSB-1500

Another aid for crossword fans, this has a cut-down (though still pretty useful) version of *Bradford's Crossword Solver's Dictionary* as well as many other features, even including an encyclopedia with proper names. This is probably the most useful of the Franklin range of electronic aids for solvers.

SETTING RECORDS

Telegraph and *Guardian* crossword setter Roger Squires is in the *Guinness Book of World Records* after setting nearly 75,000 puzzles and 2.25 million clues.

5. Electronic aids:

Apps for Tablets and Smartphones

As well as many downloadable dictionaries and thesauruses from, say, Oxford and Merriam-Webster, there are many effective and inexpensive smartphone and tablet apps on all platforms. Typing *crossword* into Google's Play store and the iPhone's equivalent will produce a good choice. As an Android user, the one I recommend is *crossword solver* by Havos Limited but there are others, normally free. The iPhone equivalents are *the crossword solver* and *crossword*, both also free.

The *Chambers Dictionary* and *Thesaurus* apps are inexpensive, comprehensive and have excellent search facilities, including wildcard searches. I have used both for years and find they are now usually my first choice as solving aids.

If you are looking for an app including free dictionary, thesaurus and word search, WordWeb, available in many formats, is the one to go for.

DID YOU KNOW?

One crossword setter in the 1960s, wishing to include the word *miniskirt* in a puzzle, found that the word had not yet been added to the *Chambers Dictionary*, and came up with this delightful clue:

'Female attire not to be found in Chambers, *but should not be looked up anyway.'*

---

6. Online dictionaries, word search and reference

If you don't have one of the electronic aids listed above, and fancy a spot of 'cheating', Collins, Oxford and Chambers all have word search facilities online. Also you may be unaware that the biggest of them all, the *Oxford English Dictionary* (the *OED*) may be available without charge online by using your local library card.

The biggest online but not necessarily the best (as it does not include some well-known dictionaries such as *Chambers*) may be at *www.onelook.com* which combines the content of over 1000 dictionaries. This passed my test using the words *keraunograph* and *taghairm* with flying colours.

For all its well-reported weaknesses in terms of reliability, Wikipedia's comprehensiveness makes it excellent if you want a quick check on a factual solution. I use it regularly as my reference of online choice and can't remember it letting me down. Rather, mistakes that have occurred in my own crosswords are likely to have arisen because I have not consulted Wikipedia.

You might also try *www.bestforpuzzles.com*, a site which has a huge variety of help tools.

The most comprehensive website for many lovers of crosswords is run by Derek Harrison in his long-running 'The Crossword Centre' at *www.crossword.org.uk*. With numerous links to other relevant sites, it has a lively message board which discusses crosswords from many different sources, albeit tilted towards the tougher crossword.There are many other websites catering for crossword enthusiasts, too many to list here.

7. *Guardian* website
Most newspapers have dedicated crossword websites but the *Guardian* website deserves a mention on its own for its easy navigability and crossword presentation including a Cheat function to gain individual letters when you're stuck. It has lots of crosswords (including those from its sister paper, the *Observer*) which can be solved online or downloaded for printing.

WHY ARE SOME CRYPTICS EASIER THAN OTHERS?
They may have more anagram clues (perhaps more than half of the total in tabloid crosswords), more hidden clues, more cross-checking in grids, more initial letters cross-checked in grids, no complex constructions, lots of short answers and no obscure ones.

8. Blogs (weblogs or daily journals): online crossword discussion groups
For anyone wanting to know why an answer is what it is, the most helpful daily blogs, contributed by teams of volunteers, are:

For the *Guardian*, *Observer*, *Financial Times*, *Independent* and *Private Eye*:
  • Type *Fifteensquared* into a search engine.

For the *Telegraph* and *Sunday Telegraph*:
  • Type *Big Dave* into a search engine.

For *The Times* and *The Sunday Times*:
  • Type *Times for the Times* into a search engine.

Unlike the others, *The Times* and *The Sunday Times* bloggers are much concerned with their solving times, usually to the nearest second, whilst commenting on what has prevented them from finishing the crossword even faster. You may find this off-putting; nevertheless in line with all other blogs, this site offers a most useful analysis of clues, normally on the day of publication.

9. Ximenes

Don't let it put you off that the next recommendation seems more
concerned with barred rather than blocked crosswords. Derrick
Macnutt's *Ximenes on the Art of the Crossword*, published first in
1966 and reprinted in 2001, is a book to learn from and enjoy. Witty
and elegant, Derek Harrison (mentioned above) has commented:
'This is far more than a treatise, it's thought-provoking and a pleasure to read.'

10. Setters unmasked

Finally, if you want to discover who lurks behind the curious
pseudonyms used by setters , either try *The A-Z of Crosswords*
(2006) by Jonathan Crowther or a more up-to-date online version
at *www.bestforpuzzles.com*. The former has the advantage of a puzzle
from each setter, chosen as the best of his or her work.

ANSWER TO SANDWICH CLUE
Pretty girl in crimson rose (8)

REBELLED – belle in red

ANSWER TO ADDITIVE CLUE
It's not a sure thing (8,7)

DEFINITE ARTICLE – definite + article

14: Practice Clues by Type

Before embarking on complete puzzles, you may wish to improve your solving skills by tackling some clues in this section. I suggest this because I have found that learners appreciate the reinforcement of the teaching hitherto by attempting clues grouped by type of clue. They are all sound and sometimes excellent examples of their kind. Many were selected as 'Clue of the Week', a long-standing feature of *The Week* magazine in which the best clue from any source is published.

The first five in each set of clues offer a little extra help and indicators are underlined in clue types which contain them. The solutions are in the Appendices, starting on page 182.

Indicators are underlined and the first five of each give extra help.

ANAGRAM CLUES

1   Fraction claimed <u>to be wrong</u> (7, first letter D)
2   Met <u>doctor</u> on train (3, 4 first letter R)
3   Hate barred <u>puzzles</u> – one gets worn out (10, first letter T)
4   Mastermind <u>rescheduled</u>, test cricket is on (6,9 first letters R & S)
5   It's nice, <u>scrambled</u> eggs (7, first letter I)
6   Choppers that may be taken out as the fleet is <u>at sea</u> (5,5)
7   Met nine or ten men I <u>somehow</u> distinguished (7)
8   Did not bid spades <u>after shuffle</u> (6)
9   Nose <u>out of joint</u> for ages (4)
10 What's wrong with Finnegan's Wake? Perhaps too <u>complicated</u> (10)

SANDWICH CLUES

1 Run in credit cheat (5, first letter T)
2 Whistle-blower <u>stops</u> work in plant (7, first letter T)
3 One in landing place is an explorer (7, first letter P)
4 On <u>entering</u> weep for close chum (5, first letter C)
5 Cook a bird <u>in</u> two ways (9, first letter M)
6 Beer <u>cans</u> beginning to bother expert (4)
7 King of England <u>holding</u> the kid, perhaps (7)
8 Spurs ground limits <u>restricting</u> United (7)
9 Crumpet may be so to speak <u>in</u> bed (8)
10 Retire <u>around</u> 50, then party! (4-3)

TAKEAWAY CLUES

1 Man at wedding <u>losing</u> ring settled for washer! (7, first letter G)
2 Signal to players left <u>out</u> of this (3, first letter C)
3 <u>Heading off</u> to sleep – like a log? (6, first letter P)
4 Drawing <u>not started</u> is a boat (5, first letter K)
5 Flat race, perhaps <u>not quite finished</u> (4, first letter E)
6 Argue when left <u>out of</u> plane journey (5)
7 Clergyman <u>overlooking</u> original crime (5)
8 Box left over is <u>incomplete</u> (4)
9 Fish <u>nibbling top off</u> seaweed (5)
10 <u>Dropping off</u> son, hit vehicle (5)

LETTER SWITCH CLUES

1 Right <u>to replace</u> leader of band for money abroad (4, first letter R)
2 Little money received from article <u>back to front</u>, (4, first letter M)
3 Irishman's apt to <u>put</u> pastor <u>first</u> (3, first letter P)
4 England's opener <u>moving down the order</u> in team is feeble (4, DOWN clue, first letter T)
5 <u>Change of</u> direction at end of dangerous river (6 first letter S)
6 Caught <u>for</u> fifty, look for England's captain (4)
7 Act of God? Conservative <u>comes forward</u> in response (8)
8 Lady Chatterley has one <u>for</u> company, for example (8)
9 Tries out jokes with time <u>for</u> judge (5)
10 Record in facilities good <u>for</u> nothing (3)

HIDDEN CLUES

1   Ethel Merman's middle name (5, first letter E)
2   Part of an address in Sloane Square (3, first letter E)
3   Brickbats in part of lake (4, first letter F)
4   Confused person found in Thames, sadly (4, first letter M)
5   Uniform packed and folded by housemaster (4, first letter S)
6   Accommodated in a hotel even though it's after ten (8)
7   Schooldays in Winchester, maybe (4)
8   Oath from odd parts of England (4)
9   In foyer, a chair – American diva's reclining, is she? (6,5)
10 Secretly getting uplift from bras or bustiers (3,4 DOWN CLUE)

REVERSAL CLUES

1   Sticky wicket's set up for spinners (4, first letter T)
2   Bar billiards shots screwed back by tip of cue (5, first letter E)
3   Put down mug on return (4, first letter L)
4   Being complacent, sticks around (4, first letter S)
5   They support conductors and help opera with backing (5, first letter P)
6   Shock from Indian government over (3)
7   Row about Italian raised (4, DOWN clue)
8   Spot a U-turn in Tory psephology (4)
9   Can egg get turned over (3)
10 Trick very large pros from the east (9)

HOMOPHONE CLUES

1   Composer in database mentioned (5, first letter L)
2   Rock songs on the radio (5, first letter A)
3   Cat heard in ruins (3, first letter R)
4   Former partner still said to be over the moon (8, first letter E)
5   Creaking sounds coming from parts of the house (9, first letter R)
6   Sound of flies and other insects (5)
7   Sound of a punch? Yes and no! (5)
8   Tropical disease – not mine by the sound of it (4)
9   Litter and bitter as mentioned (4)
10 Impose before anyone else, as comic Jackie Mason would say (5)

ALL-IN-ONE CLUES WITH VARIOUS INDICATORS

1   The last of the coal <u>in</u> bag? (5, first letter S)
2   Farewell to the French <u>about</u> to depart (5 first letter A)
3   End of skirt well up to reveal this? (5, first letter T)
4   Second me with Syria <u>in turmoil</u>? (8, first letter E)
5   Fellow likely <u>to break</u> nurse's heart? (4-6, first letter L)
6   A slave protest ending in sedition <u>being crushed</u> (8,6)
7   <u>Newly built</u> Tesco in centre of Chard? (5,5)
8   <u>Among</u> Irish, a writer (4)
9   Fail before the end of Lent? It may! (4)
10   What could <u>clobber</u> a horse and cart etc around west side of London? (7,7)

DOUBLE DEFINITION CLUES

1   Release without charge (4, first letter F)
2   Bush senior (5, first letter E)
3   Present for don (3,2 first letter P)
4   Game birds (5,3,6 first letters D,A,D)
5   Watch horse (6, first letter H))
6   Permitted or penalised (10)
7   Benjamin Roosevelt (8)
8   Book for anaesthetists? (7)
9   Of highest quality or worst (4)
10   Lawyer put in the picture (5)

CRYPTIC DEFINITION CLUES

1   Heavenly singer? (4,2,8)
2   Mater, mater (7, first letter O)
3   Device for slicing French beans (10, first letter G)
4   Man United playing away from home (9, first letter A)
5   Complaint of passenger that may involve the handling of bags (11, first letter A)
6   Site of the world's most famous listed building (4)
7   Potential birdies, maybe eagles (4)
8   Reach the same sound conclusion (5)
9   Get the bit between your teeth (5)
10   Wee Italian (6,3)

ADDITIVE CLUES

1   Most daring underwear (7, first letter B)
2   Educational establishment about to raise national standard (5,4 first letter U)
3   Go mad getting sectioned (12, first letter D)
4   Caught the supreme Diana in bad mood (5, first letter C)
5   Wash three articles abroad (7, first letter L)
6   Standard is capital (5)
7   Queen Mother meeting first lady (5)
8   Fellows at university providing list of courses (4)
9   Little man like Tony Robinson given an evening between Monday and Friday (9)
10   Furious motion of cricket bats (7-3)

NOVELTY CLUES

1   508 divided by 50, please (7, first letter D)
2   Intercity? (4, first letter B)
3   The location of love within you (5, first letter H)
4   Done the crime, now do the time (6, 7, first letters P & J)
5   _entury! (4,4,2,3)
6   Most agreeable, the Promenade des Anglais (6)
7   A,B,C,D,F,G, for example (4)
8   River Trent's edges (4)
9   As a Cockney might do with this? (3)
10   YOGDAWS? (3,5,2,10,4)

ANONYMOUS OR OTHERWISE?

In 1993 the new editor of the *New York Times* crossword immediately introduced a policy of naming his team of 'constructors'. Will Shortz decided that setters deserved to be named and besides, he thought correctly that standards would go up as a result. Editor Barbara Hall did the same a little later in the *Sunday Times*. In fact, this policy for cryptic crosswords (with pseudonyms or real names) is common to a majority of newspapers and magazines around the world including those featured in this book. Would solvers like to see setters named in say, the *Daily Mail*, *The Times* and the *Telegraph*? If my students are typical they overwhelmingly would. Could this lead to higher standards? I couldn't possibly comment!

15: Practice Puzzles

Introduction

The fifteen crosswords starting overleaf are reprinted as they appeared in their named newspapers and magazines. Setters' names, real or pseudonyms, are shown when published. They are in no special order, though the first puzzle is designed to give you a good start. All are chosen as exemplars that should reinforce the principles outlined in earlier chapters.

I think you will agree that the sight of an unfilled grid can be daunting but don't give up at the first hurdle - Mark Goodliffe, a regular and outstanding champion speed solver of *The Times* crossword, has recorded in a blog* that he scanned through a dozen or so clues in one of the competition puzzles before finding a single answer. Also remember that there is often an 'easy' way in provided by the friendly setter who, after all, does want you to complete and appreciate his or her efforts.

The solutions start on page 182, with clues repeated to avoid unnecessary page-turning. Even if you do not tackle the crosswords, close study of the annotated solutions should be rewarding.

My hope however, is that you will feel up to the solving challenge and will be surprised how many you can crack with little or no peeking at the solutions.

Please don't worry about time taken and do take a break when stuck – for the greatest pleasure, it shouldn't be a speed contest. In this connection, I once received a letter from an elderly solver saying that my Sunday crossword took him nearly the whole week to complete but he liked it that way.

Happy solving!

* You can read Mark's blog at www.piemag.com

Puzzle 1: *MoneyWeek* – Tim Moorey

The two unclued solutions (one of which is at an appropriate number) are anagrams of each other. They also both make the word given by shaded squares.

Across

1   Appropriate cut (4)
3   Device for spraying new steam iron? Not entirely (8)
9   Road eatery in which there's ecstasy? (9,4)
10 Figure from miners union a long time ahead of Labour's leader (7)
11 Indecision of daughter before break (5)
13 (3,4,6)
16 Reject former fur that's shortened (5)
18 Showing tolerance, nine let off (7)
20 Mean legislation that all balances out? (3,2,8)
21 Saucy films in airport baggage (5-3)
22 Camera accessory from Pas-de-Calais city (4)

Down

1   Angler's bottom line? (3,6)
2   Entrance for *Daily Mail* primarily (5)
4   (3,4,6)
5   Softened intros to music undermined the eastern dirge (5)
6   Dog seen in sizzling Alpine sun (7)
7   Heard what oarsmen do for eggs (3)
8   Relating to the stars in last rally (6)
12 See artist's confused formal written documents (9)
14 Set me up with energy permit (7)
15 Victory effort could be frozen (6)
17 High and mighty to fly out (5)
19 Big bird and small dog without a lead (5)
20 Leading aircraftman shortly in place (3)

Puzzle 2: *Financial Times* – Jason

Across

1 Thief's initial motive for crime (7)
5 Men in ship producing props (6)
8 What to do with this lot! (3,2,3,7)
10 Jazz fan has endless praise for neckwear (6)
11 Arcade could be costlier (8)
13 A glass vessel (8)
15 Diatribe I dropped for business (5)
17 Starting off panic is a mistake (5)
19 Letter giving pension rights? (8)
22 I generate mess? (8)
23 Spike Sprite with alcoholic drink (6)
26 Correct position of hands during fall? (3,3,5,4)
27 Journalist, after a long time succeeded in being struck off (6)
28 Frank is for keeping the Queen (7)

Down

1 Subjects run away from equatorial regions (6)
2 Bonus is over the odds – super! (5)
3 The highest possible score is a treble (7)
4 Time for two back-to-back numbers (4)
5 Something easily overlooked is shopping area font (5,5)
6 What I'd give for lolly? Extraordinary price with heartless type (7)
7 Cuff winds Bart in a bad way (9)
9 Cradles for sisters, perhaps (6)
12 Overcome by fun, decline getting drunk (10)
14 Go in after fish and chips (9)
16 Be quiet and safe on the way! (4,2)
18 Comes to a conclusion about anxieties (7)
20 Gentle child left with family under a doctor (7)
21 Dismiss the start of test on the French badger (6)
24 Marble in a doorway (5)
25 Stud's manager (4)

Puzzle 3: *Observer* – Everyman

Across

1 Pudding poorly cooked – extremely lumpy (4-4)

5 King declared war - disastrously? Not entirely (6)

9 First of players to drive, having honour (5)

10 Queen's lodged in Venice, surprisingly from then to now (4,5)

12 Crazy about a dance popular in the 1960s (5,3,5)

14 Hairstyle popular in Utah? (7)

16 Severe south wind close to coastline (7)

17 A rugby player, very large by the way (1,6)

19 Hors d'oeuvre with portion of bread, and sponge to follow (7)

21 Comedian in lace factory I scold constantly? On the contrary (5,8)

24 Female figure in Rabat in assassination (9)

25 Pole maiden has to carry at the front (5)

26 Soccer team finding time for a drink? (6)

27 Drum major's beginning to get in my punt - a lunatic (8)

Down

1 Murdoch's to produce a comic strip? (6,4)

2 The Parisian one certainly provides relaxation (7)

3 Quietly go ahead and claim (5)

4 Country line, the nicest possibly (13)

6 Ring about society girl's notice (9)

7 Sounds like a catch for a girl (7)

8 A legal document, whichever way you look at it (4)

11 Remarkable run on old bicycle (13)

13 Holding on to old lady not saying a word (7,3)

15 Elected soldier behind closed doors (2,7)

18 Rest of English giving support to turbulent priest (7)

20 Unit of explosive power – got name wrong (7)

22 18? Could get grant at university (3,2)

23 All there over in Kinmel bay (4)

Puzzle 4: *Sunday Times* – Tim Moorey

Across

1 Leave to the end tab that's for an American singer (6,7)

8 Seamen with daughter run for it (7)

9 No smooth backing in structure on bottom of ship (7)

11 Notable *Mousetrap* attraction (3,6)

12 Eastern inn used by lesser airline (5)

13 Rogue to be announced in tabloid (6)

14 Indeed so flipping unfair (3-5)

17 They could be shifting in the chase (8)

19 Composition's very good with a beat returning (6)

22 Slightly wet Chinese communist article discounted (5)

24 Forty-five right for second tenor in Italian musical foursome (7,2)

25 A cracking lodge in US city (7)

26 One terribly boring fat man (7)

27 Reformatory man to charm head of state, ER (6,7)

Down

2 Clear understanding in place for auditors (7)

3 Latrine hard work? Nothing in it with say, Ajax (9)

4 Gutted England side unexpectedly goes down the plughole (6)

5 Forsaken wild plants (3,5)

6 Thoughts of top team as getting relegated (5)

7 Charlie got better opener out without doubt (7)

8 Absurd but clear aims I put out as a writer (6,5)

10 Nothing inspires English rock singer (4,7)

15 Defeat appeared to restrict Old Testament study (5,4)

16 Major retreat in the past, for example in board game (8)

18 Commemoration: mine's in messy heap (7)

20 Start of crop area, for example could be represented as this (7)

21 Standard clothing lines on order primarily showing little colour (6)

23 Sort of pole to carry with difficulty on motorway (5)

Puzzle 5: *The Oldie* – Antico

In each across clue the wordplay omits reference to the 14 of the answer. The 14s of all across entries spell an occasion with which 14s are associated.

Across

1 Pickets prevent turning (5)

4 Brutal jibe, terribly sour (9)

9 Least sharp point by saint (7)

10 Greeting in moment brought about with English language (7)

11 One speaks furiously about leading pair of riotous pests (9)

12 Want endlessly to meet resistance? Certainly not (5)

14 See preamble (5)

16 Tooth hurt, broken by ring (5)

18 Blushing doctor rejected (3)

19 Objective editor (3)

20 Valued expensive round (5)

21 Depict quiet worker, for instance (5)

23 Unusual gear selection (5)

25 Frustrating pressure group led by bad actor (9)

28 Inactive, right away, with energy cut (7)

30 Cause of rust on taxi in bad condition (7)

31 Hours one put into musical process releasing emotions (9)

32 Composer possessed by ultimate in inspiration (5)

Down

1 Querulous in the pits, troubled (7)

2 Rocket containing new echo-sounding equipment (5)

3 Onlooker cops treat roughly (9)

4 Embargo, inhibiting to staff (5)

5 Crooks worked with top firm (4-5)

6 An enthralling story, unfamiliar (5)

7 Number in action endlessly (3)

8 Guided horse round about (7)

13 Composer from Germany seized by anger with volume rising (5)

15 Poet due to be reviewed in article (5)

16 Incomparable friend hugging companion left on ship (9)

17 Assistant, upset about error, turned up to stock up (9)

19 Despicable person, in charge after hesitation, not consistent (7)

22 Get hint, ordered to relax? On the contrary (7)

24 Plant in island filling area up (5)

26 Satellites low over north and south (5)

27 One on river going round large country (5)

29 Point about upper-class place (3)

Puzzle 6: *Independent on Sunday* – Giovanni

Across

1 Female left with desire for a bit of bacon (6)

4 Instrument in middle of craft about to plunge into planet (7)

9 One of the old people, Bill, about to enter pub (5)

10/11 Sorting out e.g. crime scenes, very quick responders handling crisis (9,8)

12 Guard left work having gone round diamonds (6)

13 Cabman with fuel running out not beginning to flap in vehicle (9)

16 Bits from the rifle put back in sack (4)

19 Haul body of guards back (4)

20 Critical times – power to kill must be curtailed (9)

22 It's distinctly possible to enjoy extremes of lunacy (6)

23 Material put forward for wild animal to eat (8)

26 Drink, grade A one, smashing! (9)

27 The last word – delete or change? (5)

28 Hostile characters chucked bits of stone (7)

29 Lord going across the street with hound (6)

Down

1 Get lost in South Africa, in China, in part of Netherlands (9)

2 Suffer at home with awful dog (5)

3 Hypocrisy associated with one beginning to lecture in church – a feature of some services (8)

4 This person and space monster get together (4)

5 Neighbourhood with awful ogre in (6)

6 State opposing issue of publication (not English) (9)

7 Type of nasty Leftie (5)

8 Act in which name sadly gets discredited (8)

14 What's on snooker table in bar (9)

15 Models no longer rather bulky – small! (8)

17 City resident beginning to enthuse when getting offer (4-5)

18 Local revamped before alteration in tea place (8)

21 Struggle to hold line in journey (6)

22 Toilet with seat not half wobbly (5)

24 Clumsy in gym having little inner energy (5)

25 Welshman's soapbox? (4)

Puzzle 7: *Guardian* – Brendan

Across

1　A name I call myself? Not quite – and wrong gender (6)

5　Violent commotions from English politician in international events (8)

9　Where snooker players compete for title, dramatically (8)

10　A party in suits, often, in Canadian city (6)

11　Stops selling record, not in use after remix (12)

13　For summer, a drop of golden sun? (4)

14　Sadly, inn's gone for modern way to announce its presence (4,4)

17　Wretched state of learner observed in strained voice (8)

18　Island going back and forth in paranoia, irrationally (4)

20　Kind of film that gets romantic chap excited (12)

23　In some cases I'm pleading innocent (6)

24　Run racket in parts of Asia, or part of Italy (8)

25　Nit-picking editor opposed to cutting inoffensive use of language (8)

26　Old man guarding a venerated object in temple (6)

Down

2　With low level of concentration, so not well done (4)

3　Pharisee at home raised fish and birds (9)

4　Religious leader wedding Jack and Elizabeth (6)

5　Movie, the scale of which is apparent in other clues (3,5,2,5)

6　Revolutionary taking over horse - a long, long way to run (8)

7　Note to follow so, for work (5)

8　Thomas is example of one that needs no tender attachment (4,6)

12　A privateer at sea, righting wrongs (10)

15　Inform about one of the little people using a needle pulling thread (9)

16　Extremely tough way Irish writer leads or Hemingway follows (8)

19　Incite prison in revolt (4,2)

21　After competition each year, a drink with jam and bread (5)

22　From within deer, a female deer (4)

Puzzle 8: *The Times* – Unnamed

Across

1 Saint knowing formality (6)
4 Spoilt loyal spouse would acknowledge this (8)
10 Hound doctor beset by poor counsel (9)
11 Not suitable if in Paris you'll return netting sure-fire winner (5)
12 Pots we hear aren't thrown (11)
14 Disregard the odds in arguing for career (3)
15 To drag one's feet around British Library is a pity (7)
17 Dressed dip with mostly mushroom as filling (6)
19 Bob, for one, locks study (6)
21 It's fine to stick around lake (7)
23 Sole parent departs (3)
24 Rat pack mixing with a hip bureaucrat (11)
26 A local office dispensing with its leader for stock holding? (5)
27 Case of drink following a mixed dish (9)
29 Such bowling hypnotized member (8)
30 Master to bring into play outside pawn (6)

Down

1 County mostly welcomes pound with anxiety (8)
2 Fling protection if initial resistance disappears (5)
3 Fleece is being worn under coat at first (3)
5 Duck fat mother's left on top (7)
6 What André has is a sweet way of speaking (5,6)
7 Tidy up behind the cooker (9)
8 Seeing lawman can start to grate (6)
9 Iron round girdle's tasselled edge (6)
13 Retailer had her bears repaired (11)
16 Wild opening group's in trailer (9)
18 Porter boxing fish, not hard to watch closely (5,3)
20 Theoretically propane explodes (2,5)
21 When time is right serviceman gets poison (6)
22 Copy Roman Catholic university's outline (6)
25 Some Apocryphal verses cut by fifty percent (5)
28 Trick one with brush (3)

Puzzle 9: *The Week* – Tim Moorey

The first letter of one down answer in each column must be omitted to form the entry. The appropriate letters thereby dropped are to be written below the grid. All answers and entries are real words and numbers in brackets refer to entries.

Across

1 Rearrange equipment restricting English judge (5)
4 A pet shoot organised in back number (9)
9 Rascal in suit falls (7)
10 One denies bit of trouble with Orange mobile (7)
11 Men's underwear from New York not right for photos (5)
12 Long time taken in Perth working on English tabloid feature (4,5)
14 Brass-making work that's of little merit? (9)
16 Volunteers a letter from Greece (5)
17 Keep bottles of white wine (5)
19 Tweet heard by sailor is second-rate (5-4)
21 Opened engaging film almost without distribution (9)
24 Look around outskirts of Rimini for a top spot (5)
26 Plunging neckline in a bolero, say leads to amorous approach (7)
28 Detective's keeping broadcast rejects (7)
29 Gate in ground lets in Rugby Union team initially (9)
30 Name for 500 stylish men, people barely seen (5)

Down

1 Follows run in stitches (5)
2 Nice sauce taken by all there recently released (4,3)
3 Former PM left to inspire young man on street (9)
4 Having an advantage, new German goes into work (3-2)
5 College board no good (3)
6 Nothing new for doctor in water shortage (5)
7 High tea includes celebrity, a goddess (7)
8 One's high on punch but journalist keeps sober surprisingly (9)
13 Eat a lot of Cheddar? (5)
14 Candidate put on last broadcast (9)
15 Put down in French square close to boulevard (5)
16 What many Ascot gentlemen have for somebody (3,6)
18 Hampshire town supporting hospital transfer (7)
20 Harry or Andrew contracted (7)
22 Uniform leads to terribly stuffy competitions (5)
23 Avoid a large American car (5)
25 Baker's supply indeed containing a stone (5)
27 Biblical high priest's story: the last shall be first (3)

Puzzle 10: *The i Newspaper* – DAC

Across

1   Recalled a celebration mass in Spanish port (6)

4   Urgent job once grapes are picked? (8)

9   Smoke rings forbidden (5)

10 In most of island people accepted wage rise (9)

11 In Natal get lost, deviating from course (10)

12 Test shortened for a learner (4)

14 Obtain most offensive German article about radical writer (8,5)

16 Various irons too light for one interested in birdies? (13)

18 Duck leaves lake (4)

19 Member of Oasis taking part in pop congress? (10)

22 I'll treat lawn, one with nasty mark left by wild fire (9)

23 African dictator introducing order, in a manner of speaking (5)

24 A river goes through city, one in Scotland (8)

25 Animated character full of cold (6)

Down

1   New York opera's suppressing old time pieces of music (6)

2   Country exiling an '80s singer (2,3)

3   Travels to Brest as arranged following journey across Channel at last (10)

5   Two causes of disaster in the main for a musician (4,3,6)

6   Twist a lot (4)

7   I get close to home showing determination (2,7)

8   Enjoy friendly relations? Piffle (3,5)

10 Maybe how I've got trainer repaired (13)

13 Guess I'm stuck in English Channel (10)

14 Soldier meets new friend at top watering hole (3,6)

15 Noble precursor of Labour's ISA (8)

17 Short, thickset and fox-y? (6)

20 Frenchman turned green before end of voyage (5)

21 Rear female animal (4)

Puzzle 11: *Oxford Times* – Colin Dexter

Across

1 There'll be times when you do this (8)

5 Still causing interference (6)

10 A relative who owns a porn shop, so to speak (5)

11 Cut off – not dat limb, though (9)

12 Poor Dad is in a contemptuous mood (7)

13 You need to rake last of leafage piling up from this (3,4)

14 Picked up by devil? Not an accurate shot, mind! (8)

16 A bowler who may get a duck? (5)

19 In combat? Hostile swordsman (5)

21 What a pension will surely give you in retirement (8)

24 A name with micro waves? (7)

26 Tea before noon gives you wind (7)

27 Losing cat can make one so sentimental (9)

28 Arch beggar's plea? (5)

29 Lion always follows this sign (6)

30 Gave evidence when a terrorist leader gets tried (8)

Down

1 Like my old last bit of gateau, possibly (6)

2 One who has a key role to play (9)

3 Place that's white and clean, I'd suspect (7)

4 Left with a burden? Not half! (5)

6 Walked with half tremor, on tossing deck (7)

7 Underground bit of rhizome (5)

8 Armour for CO, right? Tempered steel (8)

9 Theatrical star does like chocolates (8)

15 This – or Cam-ford, perhaps? (8)

17 It's a man to cut up (9)

18 Phil makes this orchestra melodious (8)

20 Space for so much furniture could be so great (7)

22 Work in hotel abroad is A1 (3-4)

23 Really venomous denied (6)

25 If matted, rinse in turps (5)

26 You'll find us leaving historian speechless (5)

Puzzle 12: *Daily Telegraph* – Unnamed

Across

1 Presumably it can't be played by an orchestra in front of the stage? (10,5)
9 Tom's representative inside has some cheese (9)
10 Plate of fish (5)
11 Made possible being competent in the finish (7)
12 Talk of nothing, say, but a large French country-house (7)
13 Utilise sheep, we hear (3)
14 How policemen operate in great numbers (2,5)
17 One making many a cut on the farm (7)
19 Left in Connecticut with American medicine (7)
22 Given a turn by a driver? (7)
24 Part of the theatre that is mine (3)
25 Try to cope with small weight of fruit (7)
26 Cheese lady had going round the small house (7)
28 Most upset it had been split (3-2)
29 Curiously I can't tire although it is very complicated (9)
30 Beastly swimmer that might be found in Scotland? (4,4,7)

Down

1 New biological trace, it's concerned with the science of microscopic organisms (15)
2 Short break during the sentence (5)
3 Better find a good walker (7)
4 Late on payment (7)
5 Reviews new section (7)
6 Mother's wise having this treatment (7)
7 Not a leader of fashion in the field! (9)
8 Ups and downs of a professional chess player? (9,6)
15 Extravagantly fanciful sort of fast antic (9)
16 Said gang found at French vineyard (3)
18 An involuntary contraction from a chicken (3)
20 Almost stopping absurd movement of cricket ball (7)
21 Old Bob needs other pieces to make a group (7)
22 Rat must emerge from the rock layer (7)
23 Courtin' disaster leading to uproar (7)
27 A health-giving drink (5)

Puzzle 13: *Sunday Telegraph* – Unnamed

Across

7 On course, performing rather well or rather poorly (5,3)

9 Jack's appearing in operatic part in Lawrence's place (6)

10 Some tigers at zoo not the real thing (6)

11 Rip off, in a word, someone who's reckless (8)

12 For example, football magazine's linked with Liverpool, say (9,5)

15 Island with a lot of dance (4)

17 What's repeatedly found in grizzly bear, possibly, or other wild animal (5)

19 Flamboyance – it's not a word that can be seen in this clue (4)

20 Western crew showering after time for strenuous exercise (6,8)

23 Wrongly perceived young woman in front of crowd, speaking (8)

25 Interfere with person who's entitled to hold key (6)

27 Scotch is what drunken revellers try, initially (6)

28 Remove two wives, with a third mistreated inside (8)

Down

1 European carried by rail coming to Paddington, say (4)

2 Pieced together picture of ancient lawgiver (6)

3 Misbehaving youngster, intermittently aberrant (4)

4 Caught, unfortunately, outside one Channel port (6)

5 I pardon a wrong, harbouring unreasonable suspicions (8)

6 Politically co-operative oil company retaining current skilled worker (10)

8 Flamboyancy Scrabble player can never produce (7)

13 Kind of author that takes gamble with flier, originally (10)

14 Final notice about monarch's round-the-world trip (5)

16 Islander's at home, nursing his arm that's broken (8)

18 Not for touching (7)

21 Sporting and jovial male having aesthetic interests (6)

22 Insignificant type's critical comment on wine (6)

24 Blue swallow (4)

26 Be first to play heavy metal? Doesn't sound like it (4)

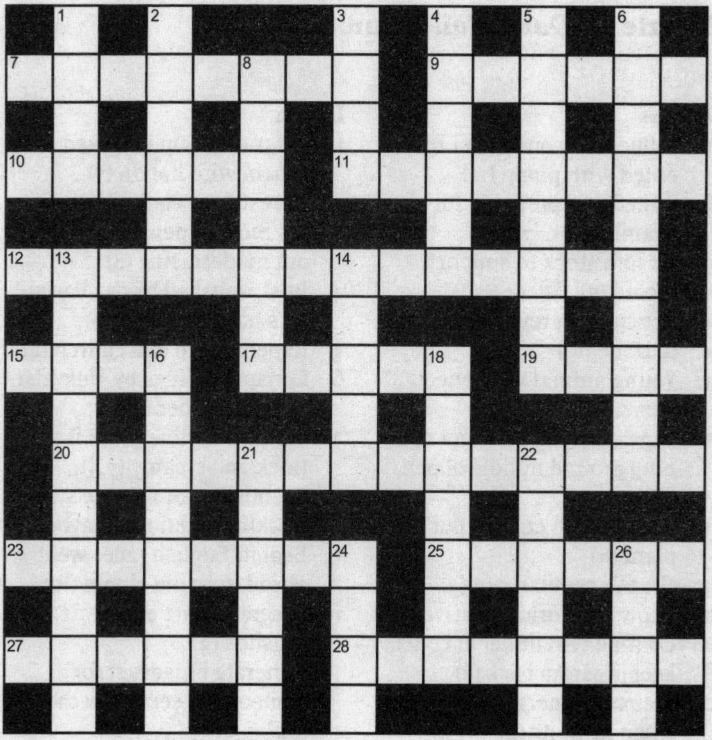

Puzzle 14: *Daily Mail* – Unnamed

Across

1 Influential condition Elgar noted with pomp (12)

8 Edited and prepared for examination (7)

9 Unsold stock to support record (7)

11 Article men rewrite relating to trade (10)

12 Young animal with one chrysalis (4)

14 Type of swine a danger running around middle of pen (8)

16 Old Spanish change put into plant (6)

17 Grant's regular gun (3)

19 Show off Florida relative (6)

21 Confine remainder at court, keeping Irish back (8)

24 Source of energy at home when he quits (4)

25 Speak once (badly) about good old birthday treat (6,4)

27 Mark grabs money, a lasting power (7)

28 Knot resolved in daring cut with middle of sword (7)

29 US docker rearranged organs on helm (12)

Down

1 Vicar turns up in mixed school with hat on (7)

2 Rarest tuna cooked here? (10)

3 It's more expensive going out modernising (8)

4 Bust smashed by the Parisian's hard to detect (6)

5 Expert's rare in a church (4)

6 Conspire – lines by Unionist put into cipher (7)

7 Fancy farm foie gras? It's thick and creamy (7,5)

10 Promising rain-gauge's working about ten maybe (12)

13 Beat it; English races went ahead in rising gloom (10)

15 Essential part of cereals, crushed (3)

18 Generate broadcast for someone in second decade (8)

20 Head off chaos at a party of green hue (7)

22 I get stuck into translating a Latin language (7)

23 Prominently display Spanish whip (6)

26 Faction's victory over government (4)

16: Leaving the Best Till Last

Of all the crosswords that I have used on my workshops, this over-leaf puzzle by Virgilius in the *Independent* is the one that students admire and enjoy the most.

The Best Puzzle: *Independent* – Virgilius

Across

5   Green light around a tree (3)

7   Cruel conflict holds it back (7)

9   One of the parrots – some talk easily (3)

10 Joins together to repel something foul (5)

11 For example, origin of goose (3)

12 Coats of many colours? (5)

13 Heavens above! The monarch's put outside (5)

15 Helps cure wrong in grave situation (9)

18 More work – that's ideal (6)

19 Former copper's energy let off (6)

20 Corrupt man copied lots of games (9)

21 Left with old ship for slow passage (5)

23 Servant's farewell takes little time (5)

25 This bed's mine (3)

26 Thrash one in school (5)

27 Sailor who abandons sinking ship? Just the opposite (3)

28 City-state (3,4)

29 Drink with sympathetic companion? (3)

Down

1   Bird that is a fledgling (6)

2   Antipodean state that sounds like a monarchy (10)

3   Ruler providing good support for the family (4)

4   Piece of Englishman's residence? (6)

6   At length irk PM badly, as member of old order (6,7)

7   Note is to be played again (3)

8   Hard work put into dance (3)

9   Medieval adventurers organised in ten ranks? Right (7,6)

14 Indian money in Peru changed by European (5)

16 Pressure on amusing person as safeguard (10)

17 Watering hole used by natives (5)

20 South American rodent grabs it for a hole (6)

22 Partners in love? No, it's not reciprocal (3-3)

24 Preserve money (3)

25 Vessel carrying wine, primarily hock (4)

26 Pot from East or West acceptable (3)

17: Which Crosswords Next?

At the end of my workshops, I give suggestions as to which nationally available blocked puzzles students might try after the course, taking account of solving difficulty and pleasure. It's a list that hasn't changed much for several years. Of course, assessment of difficulty levels varies between assessors but this is mine. Also, whether intended by editors or not, the Monday puzzle in the *Daily Telegraph*, *Guardian* and *The Times* may well be a little easier than for the rest of the week and this has to be taken into account.

The **starred bands** below are what I perceive to be the approximate order of their difficulty. Crosswords within each group are also in increasing levels of difficulty, though this is even more subjective.

Many of these puzzles are available online, some of them free or requiring a small payment.

* DAILY MIRROR, DAILY STAR, THE SUN AND THEIR SUNDAY SISTERS

Ximenean principles are sometimes stretched in this group; they have considerably more anagrams and hidden clues than others. Their answer words are straightforward; literary, art and musical references are few. Grids may have fewer than average blocked squares, increasing cross-checking possibilities and some answers may be fully 'checked', such that solvers can find an answer appearing without having solved the clue. Most of these crosswords have two sets of clues (cryptic and non-cryptic) for the same grid, a feature that's really valued by complete beginners.

** DAILY MAIL, MAIL ON SUNDAY, DAILY EXPRESS, SUNDAY EXPRESS, DAILY TELEGRAPH

These all follow Ximenean principles to a large extent. Many would probably agree that the *Telegraph* has the highest proportion of distinctive clues, though the others all have loyal, satisfied solvers.

*** OBSERVER EVERYMAN, SUNDAY TELEGRAPH, FINANCIAL TIMES, THE OLDIE GENIUS, THE WEEK, THE SUNDAY TIMES, INDEPENDENT, THE I NEWSPAPER, INDEPENDENT ON SUNDAY, DAILY TELEGRAPH TOUGHIE, PRIVATE EYE

This large group is the one in which difficulty level varies the most. Most of them will include clues with topical references. One or two lesser-known words may well be included and there can be some stretching of definitional meanings. Incidentally, the *i newspaper* currently republishes past crosswords from its sister, the *Independent*. Note that these two, the *Daily Telegraph* Toughie, *Financial Times* and *Sunday Times* have more than one setter which inevitably leads to more variability, but also more loyalty to individual setters. Apart from the *Sunday Telegraph*, all these publications name their setters, using pseudonyms or real names.

**** TIMES, GUARDIAN

These two also have a panel of setters, named in the *Guardian* but not in *The Times*. Day-by-day difficulty levels can vary considerably, sometimes being close to the three star group, other days a long way from that. A *Guardian* poll showed that solvers are happy with this, most voting for an occasional very tough challenge and that is probably true for *Times* solvers. The more complex constructions referred to in Chapter 9 may make the occasional appearance in both of these two puzzles.

The *Guardian* crossword has a number of setters whose clues are further away from Ximenes than any other daily newspaper. That's not to pass judgment on quality or enjoyment – it is to say that potential solvers following this book will find they need to think laterally and more deeply than for the other crosswords. However, familiarity with each setter's tricks does of course help considerably. The *Guardian*'s Araucaria, who died in November 2013, was in a special category of his own as being both proudly non-Ximenean and much loved, especially for his original themes and long anagrams. He is also the only setter so far to have received the MBE and to have made an appearance on *Desert Island Discs*. His puzzles are still available in book form and online.

What people want in addition are recommendations for those that might give extra pleasure and are at the easiest end of the solving range in their newspapers.

Not including my own puzzles and recognising that this is highly subjective, I recommend this elite group, based not only on workshop participant feedback but also on the ultimate test of which setters cause me to buy the newspaper in question:

Not only do these conform fully to the teaching outlined in this book, they usually offer smooth surface meanings and ingenious wordplay. For those wanting themes (and I'm aware that some solvers do not), the *Oldie* is always themed with a preamble. The Virgilius and Brendan puzzles are also nearly always themed, albeit that the theme may not be apparent until the end.

In a category of its own, with regularly brilliant puzzles, is *The Times* including its weekend Jumbo crossword, though I hesitate to make a specific regular daily recommendation as difficulty levels vary quite a lot and its many setters are unnamed.

PART 4

APPENDICES

> 'How clean is your house? Meet the crossword fanatic who has not
> cleaned her flat for 24 years.'
> Channel 4 TV Listings

1. Abbreviations

This list includes the most common crossword abbreviations and
all of those used in this book's clues and puzzles. To assist solvers, it is arranged in order of the abbreviated word rather than the
abbreviation itself.

a	A	breadth	B	daughter	D
about	A, C,	British	B,BR	day	D
	CA,	British Lib.	BL	delete	D
	RE	brown	BR	departs	D
abstemious	TT	bye	B	died	D
ace	A			diamonds	D
adult	A	caught	C	doctor	DR,
against	V	century	C		MO,
ambassador	HE	chapter	C, CH		MB
American	A, US	church	CE,	duke	D
answer	A		CH	Dutch	D
are	A	circle	O		
arrived	ARR	city	EC,	east(ern)	E
area	A		LA,	each year	PA
artist	RA		NY	ecstasy	E
		clubs	C	energy	E
bachelor	B	cold	C	engineers	RE
bill	AC	companion	CH	English	E
bishop	B,	Conservative	C	European	E
	RR	copper	CU		
black	B	court	CT	father	FR
Bob	B	cross	X	female	F
book	B,	current	I, AC	fifty	L
	VOL		DC	fighter	F
born	B			fine	F
bowled	B	date	D	first person	A

five	V	Judge	J	navy	N,
five hundred	D				RN
following	F	key	see	new	N
former	EX		note	New Testament	
force	F, G	king	K, R		NT
forte	F	King Edward	ER	newton	N
frequency	F	kiss	X	nitrogen	N
		knight	K, N	noon	N
gallons	G			north(ern)	N
Germany	G	lake	L	note	A-G,
good	G	large	L		DO(H),
government	G	lawman	DA		RE,
graduate	MA,	lead	PB		MI,
	BA,	learner	L		FA(H),
	MBA	left	L		SO(H),
grand	G	Liberal	L		LA(H),
gunners	RA	line	L		TI
		litre	L	nothing	O
hard	H	lost	L	nought	O
has	S	loud	F		
hearts	H	love	O	of, old	O
height	H			old Bob	S
Henry	H	maiden	M	Old Testament	
heroin	H	male	M		OT
Her (or His)		mark(s)	M	one	A, I
Majesty	HR	married	M		or UN
horse	H	masculine	M	order	O, OM
hospital	H	mass	M	other ranks	OR
hot	H	mile	M	oxygen	O
hour	H, HR	million(s)	M		
house	HO	minute(s)	M	page	P
hundred	C	model	T	parking	P
husband	H	monarch	ER, R	painter	RA
hydrogen	H	Monsieur	M	partners	EW,
		motorway	M,		NS
in charge	IC		MI	pawn	P
Irish	IR	mount	MT	penny, pence	P
iron	FE			piano	P
is	S	name	N	point	N, S,
island	I	National Theatre			E, W
			NT	politician	MP
Jack	J, AB	posh	U		

potassium	K	shirt	T	unknown	X, Y,
pound	L	sign of error	X		Z
power	P	silver	AG	upper-class	U
pressure	P	singular	S		
		small	S	versus	V
quarter	N, S,	society	S	very	V
	E, W	soldier	GI	very large	OS
queen	Q, R,	son	S	very loud	FF
	ER,	south(ern)	S	very quiet	PP
	HM	spades	S	victory	V
question	Q,	Spain	E	volts	V
	QU	Spanish	SP	volume	V
quiet(ly)	P, SH	special	S	volunteer	TA
		spies	CIA	vote	X
race(s)	TT	square	S		
radical	R	stone	ST	watts	W
rare	R	street	ST	way	AVE,
resistance	R	student	L		MI,
right	R	succeeded	S		RD,
river	R	Switzerland	CH		ST
ring	O			weight	W
road	RD	tango	T	west(ern)	W
road junction	T	tee	T	wicket	W
Roman Catholic		temperature	T	wide	W
	RC	ten	X	width	W
rook	R	tenor	T	wife	W
round	O	tense	T	with	W
run(s)	R	thousand	K, M	women's	W
		time	T	work	OP
sailor	AB	ton(s)	T		
saint	S, ST	turn	U	yard	Y
seaman	AB			year(s)	Y
second(s)	S	Unionist	U	yen	Y
see	V, C	united	U		
sergeant	DS	universal	U	zero	O
ship	SS	university	U		

2. Solutions: Practice Clues by Type

In the following two sections of annotated solutions, letters that form anagrams (anagram fodder), are shown by an asterisk, definitions are *italicised* and indicators are underlined.

ANAGRAM CLUES

1	*Fraction* claimed to <u>be wrong</u> **claimed***	DECIMAL
2	*Met* <u>doctor</u> on train **on train***	RAN INTO
3	Hate barred <u>puzzles</u> – one gets *worn out* **hate barred***	THREADBARE
4	*Mastermind* <u>rescheduled</u>, test cricket is on **test cricket is on***	ROCKET SCIENTIST
5	It's nice, <u>scrambled</u> *eggs* **its nice***	INCITES
6	*Choppers that may be taken out* as the fleet is at sea **as the fleet***	FALSE TEETH
7	Met nine or ten men I <u>somehow</u> *distinguished* **met nine*** and **ten mine I*** (double anagram)	EMINENT
8	*Did not bid* spades <u>after shuffle</u> **spades***	PASSED
9	Nose <u>out of joint</u> for *ages* **nose***	EONS
10	*What's wrong with Finnegan's Wake?* Perhaps too <u>complicated</u> **perhaps too***	APOSTROPHE

SANDWICH CLUES

1	Run <u>in</u> credit *cheat* (**r** in **tick**)	TRICK
2	Whistle-blower <u>stops</u> work in *plant* (**ref** in **toil**)	TREFOIL
3	One <u>in</u> landing place *is an explorer* (**one** in **pier**)	PIONEER

4	On <u>entering</u> weep for *close chum* (**on** in **cry**)	CRONY
5	*Cook* a bird <u>in</u> two ways (**crow** in **M1** and **Ave.**)	MICROWAVE
6	Beer <u>cans</u> beginning to bother *expert* (**b** in **ale**)	ABLE
7	King of England <u>holding</u> the *kid, perhaps* (**the** in **Lear**)	LEATHER
8	*Spurs* ground limits <u>restricting</u> United (**U** in **limits***)	STIMULI
9	*Crumpet may be so* to speak <u>in</u> bed (**utter** in **bed**)	BUTTERED
10	Retire <u>around</u> 50, then *party!* (**l** in **bow out**)	BLOW-OUT

TAKEAWAY CLUES

1	Man at wedding <u>losing</u> ring settled for *washer!* (**groom** minus **o** plus **met**)	GROMMET
2	*Signal to players* left <u>out</u> of this (**clue** minus **l**)	CUE
3	<u>Heading off</u> to sleep – *like a log?* (**slumber** minus **s**)	LUMBER
4	Drawing <u>not started</u> is *a boat* (**sketch** minus **s**)	KETCH
5	*Flat* race, perhaps <u>not quite finished</u> (**event** minus **t**)	EVEN
6	*Argue* when left <u>out of</u> plane journey (**flight** minus **l**)	FIGHT
7	Clergyman <u>overlooking</u> original *crime* (**parson** minus **p**)	ARSON
8	*Box* left over is <u>incomplete</u> (**spare** minus **e**)	SPAR
9	*Fish* <u>nibbling top off</u> seaweed (**tangle** minus **t**)	ANGLE
10	<u>Dropping off</u> son, hit *vehicle* (**strike** minus **s**)	TRIKE

LETTER SWITCH CLUES

1	Right to <u>replace</u> leader of band for *money abroad* (**band** with **r** replacing **b**)	RAND
2	*Little money* received from article <u>back to front</u> (**item** with **m** moved to first place)	MITE
3	*Irishman*'s apt to <u>put</u> pastor <u>first</u> (**apt** with **p** moved to first place)	PAT
4	England's opener <u>moving down the order</u> in team is *feeble* (**team** with **e** moved to end, a **down** clue)	TAME
5	<u>Change of direction</u> at end of dangerous *river* (**severe** with final **e** replaced by **n**)	SEVERN
6	Caught <u>for</u> fifty, look for *England's captain* (**c** for **l** in **look**)	COOK
7	*Act of God?* Conservative <u>comes forward</u> in response (**reaction** with **c** moved left)	CREATION
8	Lady Chatterley has one <u>for</u> company, for *example* (**Constance** with **i** for **Co.**)	INSTANCE
9	*Tries out* jokes with time <u>for</u> judge (**t** for **j** in **jests**)	TESTS
10	*Record* in facilities good <u>for</u> nothing (**g** for **o** in **loo**)	LOG

HIDDEN CLUES

1	Ethel Merman<u>'s</u> middle *name* (middle of Eth**el Mer**man)	ELMER
2	*Part of an address* <u>in</u> Sloane Square (inside Sloan**e Sq**uare)	ESQ
3	*Brickbats* <u>in</u> part of lake (inside o**f lak**e)	FLAK
4	*Confused person* <u>found in</u> Thames, sadly (inside Tha**mes s**adly)	MESS
5	*Uniform* <u>packed and folded</u> by housemaster	SAME

(inside hous**emas**ter reversed)

6	<u>Accommodated in</u> a hotel even though *it's after ten* (inside hot**el even** though)	ELEVENTH
7	*Schooldays* <u>in</u> Winchester, maybe (inside Winches**ter m**aybe)	TERM
8	*Oath* <u>from</u> odd parts of England (**England** minus alternate letters)	EGAD
9	<u>In</u> foyer, a chair – American diva's <u>reclining</u>, *is she?* (inside fo**yer, a chair – Am**erican reversed)	MARIAH CAREY
10	*Secretly* getting <u>uplift from</u> bras or bustiers (reversed inside br**as or bus**tiers)	SUB ROSA

REVERSAL CLUES

1	Sticky wicket's <u>set up</u> for *spinners* (reversed **spot**; a **down** clue)	TOPS
2	*Bar* billiards shots <u>screwed back</u> by tip of cue (**e** plus reversed **pots**)	ESTOP
3	*Put down* mug <u>on return</u> (reversed **dial** = **face**)	LAID
4	*Being complacent*, sticks <u>around</u> (reversed **gums**)	SMUG
5	*They support conductors* and help opera with <u>backing</u> (reversed **aid op**)	PODIA
6	*Shock* from Indian government <u>over</u> (reversed **Raj**)	JAR
7	*Row* about Italian <u>raised</u> (reversed **re it**)	TIER
8	*Spot* <u>a U-turn</u> in Tory psephology (reversed inside Tor**y pse**phology)	ESPY
9	*Can* egg get <u>turned over</u> (reversed **nit**)	TIN
10	*Trick* very large pros <u>from the east</u> (reversed **mega tarts**)	STRATAGEM

HOMOPHONE CLUES

1	*Composer* in database <u>mentioned</u> (sounds like **list**)	LISZT
2	*Rock* songs <u>on the radio</u> (sounds like **airs**)	AYERS
3	*Cat* <u>heard</u> in ruins (sounds like **wrecks**)	REX
4	Former partner still <u>said to be</u> *over the moon* (sounds like **ex static**)	ECSTATIC
5	*Creaking* <u>sounds</u> coming from parts of the house (sounds like **room attic**)	RHEUMATIC
6	<u>Sound</u> of flies and *other insects* (sounds like **flees**)	FLEAS
7	<u>Sound</u> *of a punch?* Yes and no! (sounds like **nay**)	NEIGH
8	*Tropical disease* – not mine <u>by the sound of</u> it (sounds like **yours**)	YAWS
9	*Litter* and bitter <u>as mentioned</u> (sounds like **beer**)	BIER
10	*Impose* before anyone else, as comic Jackie Mason <u>would say</u> (sounds like **first**)	FOIST

ALL-IN-ONE CLUES WITH VARIOUS INDICATORS

1	*The last of the coal* <u>in</u> bag? (**l** in **sack**)	SLACK
2	*Farewell to the French* <u>about</u> to depart (**die** in **au**)	ADIEU
3	*End of skirt well up to reveal this?* (**t** plus **high**)	THIGH
4	*Second me with Syria* <u>in turmoil?</u> (**s me Syria***)	EMISSARY
5	*Fellow likely* <u>to break</u> *nurse's heart?* (**lad** plus **likely*** plus **r**)	LADY-KILLER
6	*A slave protest ending in sedition* <u>being crushed</u> (**a slave protest n***)	PEASANTS REVOLT

7	<u>Newly built</u> *Tesco in centre of Chard*? (**Tesco** in **har***)	CHAIN STORE
8	<u>Among</u> *Irish, a writer* (inside Iri**sh a w**riter)	SHAW
9	*Fail before the end of Lent? It may!* (**die** plus **t**)	DIET
10	*What could <u>clobber</u> a horse and cart etc around west side of London?* (**L** in **a horse cart etc***)	CHELSEA TRACTOR

DOUBLE DEFINITION CLUES

1	*Release without charge*	FREE
2	*Bush senior*	ELDER
3	*Present for don*	PUT ON
4	*Game birds*	DUCKS AND DRAKES
5	*Watch horse*	HUNTER
6	*Permitted or penalised*	SANCTIONED
7	*Benjamin Roosevelt*	FRANKLIN
8	*Book for anaesthetists?*	NUMBERS
9	*Of highest quality or worst*	BEST
10	*Lawyer put in the picture*	BRIEF

CRYPTIC DEFINITION CLUES

1	*Heavenly singer?*	BIRDS OF PARADISE
2	*Mater, mater*	OEDIPUS
3	*Device for slicing French beans* (**bean** = **head**)	GUILLOTINE
4	*Man United playing away from home* (**united** = **married**)	ADULTERER
5	*Complaint of passenger that may involve the handling of bags*	AIRSICKNESS
6	*Site of the world's most famous listed building*	PISA
7	*Potential birdies, maybe eagles*	EGGS
8	*Reach the same sound conclusion*	RHYME
9	*Get the bit between your teeth*	FLOSS
10	*Wee Italian*	NUMERO UNO

ADDITIVE CLUES

1	*Most daring* underwear (**bra** + **vest**)	BRAVEST
2	Educational establishment about to raise *national standard* (**uni** + **on** + **jack**)	UNION JACK
3	Go mad getting *sectioned* (**depart** + **mental**)	DEPARTMENTAL
4	Caught the supreme Diana *in bad mood* (**c** + **Ross**)	CROSS
5	*Wash* three articles abroad (**la un der**)	LAUNDER
6	Standard is *capital* (**par is**)	PARIS
7	*Queen* Mother meeting first lady (**ma** + **Eve**)	MAEVE
8	Fellows at university providing *list of courses* (**men** + **u**)	MENU
9	Little man like Tony Robinson given *an evening between Monday and Friday* (**wee knight**)	WEEKNIGHT
10	*Furious* motion of cricket bats (**hopping** + **mad**)	HOPPING MAD

NOVELTY CLUES (SOME NOT XIMENEAN)

1	508 divided by 50, *please* (**l** in **d eight**)	DELIGHT
2	*Intercity?* (**inter** and **city**)	BURY
3	*The location of love within you* (**love** = **o**, central letter of **you**)	HEART
4	*Done the crime, now do the time*	POETIC JUSTICE
5	–entury (**century** minus **c**)	LONG TIME NO SEE
6	*Most agreeable*, the Promenade des Anglais (**Nice St**)	NICEST

7	A, B, C, D, F, G, for example (**not E**)	NOTE
8	*River* Trent's edges (first and last letters of **Trent**)	TEES
9	*As a Cockney might do with this?* ('**ear**)	EAR
10	YOGDAWS? **OGD*** in **YAWS***	GOD MOVES IN MYSTERIOUS WAYS

3. Solutions: Practice Puzzles

Puzzle 1: MoneyWeek

Across

1 *Appropriate cut*
double definition
NICK (verb appropriate)

3 *Device for spraying* <u>new</u> steam iron? <u>Not entirely</u>
anagram incl. takeaway
ATOMISER – steam iro(n)*

9 *Roadside eatery in which there's ecstasy?*
cryptic definition
TRANSPORT CAFÉ

10 *Figure* from miners union a long time ahead of Labour's leader
additive
NUMERAL – NUM + era + L

11 *Indecision* of daughter before break
additive
DRIFT – d + rift

13 ONE PLUS TWELVE – two plus eleven* (= thirteen)

16 *Reject* former fur that's <u>shortened</u>
additive incl. takeaway

EXPEL – ex + pel(t)

18 *Showing tolerance,* nine let <u>off</u>
anagram
LENIENT – nine let*

20 *Mean legislation that all balances out?*
cryptic definition
LAW OF AVERAGES

21 *Saucy films* in *airport baggage*
double definition
CARRY-ONS

22 *Camera accessory* from *Pas-de-Calais city*
double definition
LENS

Down

1 *Angler's bottom line?*
cryptic definition
NET INCOME

2 *Entrance* for Daily Mail primarily
additive
CHARM – char + M

4 TWO PLUS ELEVEN – one plus twelve* (= thirteen)

5 *Softened* intros to music undermined the eastern dirge
additive
MUTED – initial letters

6 *Dog* seen in <u>sizzling</u> Alpine sun
anagram
SPANIEL – Alpine S*

7 <u>Heard</u> what oarsmen do for *eggs*
homophone
ROE – sounds like row

8 *Relating to the stars in* l<u>ast ral</u>ly
hidden
ASTRAL

12 See artist's <u>confused</u> *formal written documents*
anagram

TREATISES – see artist*

14 Set me <u>up</u> with energy *permit*
additive incl. reversal (down clue)
EMPOWER – reversed me + power

15 Victory effort could be *frozen*
additive
WINTRY – win try

17 *High and mighty* to fly <u>out</u>
anagram
LOFTY – to fly*

19 *Big bird* and small dog <u>without</u> a lead
takeaway
EAGLE – (b)eagle

20 *Leading aircraftman* shortly <u>in</u> place
hidden
LAC

Puzzle 2: Financial Times

Across

1 Thief's initial motive for *crime*
additive
TREASON – T + reason

5 Men <u>in</u> ship producing *props*
sandwich
SCREWS – crew inside SS = ship

8 *What to do with this lot!*
cryptic definition
PUT UP FOR AUCTION

10 Jazz fan <u>has</u> endless praise for *neckwear*
sandwich
CRAVAT – rav(e) inside cat

11 *Arcade* <u>could be</u> costlier

anagram
CLOISTER – costlier*

13 *A glass vessel*
double definition
SCHOONER

15 Diatribe I <u>dropped</u> for *business*
takeaway
TRADE – tirade less i

17 Starting <u>off</u> panic is *a mistake*
takeaway
ERROR – terror less T

19 *Letter giving pension rights?*
cryptic definition
LANDLADY – pension = boarding house

22 *I generate mess?*
   anagram all-in-one
   TEENAGER – generate*
23 *Spike* Sprite with alcoholic
   drink
   additive
   IMPALE – imp + ale
26 *Correct position of hands
   during fall?*
   cryptic definition
   PUT THE CLOCK BACK –
   fall = autumn
27 Journalist, after a long time
   succeeded in being *struck off*
   additive
   ERASED – era + s + ed.
28 *Frank* is for <u>keeping</u> the Queen
   sandwich
   SINCERE – ER in since

Down
1 *Subjects* run <u>away</u> from
   equatorial regions
   takeaway
   TOPICS – t(r)opics
2 *Bonus is over the odds – super!*
   triple definition
   EXTRA
3 *The highest possible score is a
   treble*
   double definition
   SOPRANO
4 *Time* for two <u>back-to-back</u>
   numbers
   reversal
   NOON – no + no reversed
5 *Something easily overlooked* is
   shopping area font
   additive
   SMALL PRINT – 's + mall +
   print
6 *What I'd give for lolly?*
   <u>Extraordinary</u> price with
   <u>heartless</u> type
   anagram incl. takeaway
   RECEIPT – price t(yp)e*
7 *Cuff* winds Bart <u>in a bad way</u>
   anagram
   WRISTBAND – winds Bart*
9 *Cradles* for *sisters, perhaps*
   double definition
   NURSES
12 *Overcome* by fun, decline
   <u>getting drunk</u>
   anagram
   INFLUENCED – fun decline*
14 Go in after fish and *chips*
   additive
   CARPENTER – carp + enter
16 *Be quiet and safe on the way!*
   double definition
   BELT UP – way = road
18 *Comes to a conclusion* about
   anxieties
   additive
   REACHES – re + aches
20 *Gentle child* left with family
   under a doctor
   additive
   LAMBKIN – L + a MB + kin
21 <u>Dismiss the start of</u> test on
   the French *badger*
   additive incl. takeaway
   HECKLE – (c)heck + le
24 *Marble* in a doorway
   additive
   AGATE – a + gate
25 *Stud's manager*
   double definition
   BOSS

Puzzle 3: Observer Everyman

Across

1 *Pudding* poorly <u>cooked</u> –
<u>extremely</u> lumpy
anagram incl. additive
ROLY-POLY – poorly* +
l(ump)y

5 *King* declar**ed war** – **d**isas-
trously? <u>Not entirely</u>
hidden
EDWARD

9 First of players to drive,
having honour
additive
PRIDE – p + ride

10 Queen's <u>lodged in</u> Venice,
<u>surprisingly</u> *from then to now*
sandwich incl. anagram
EVER SINCE – ER's inside
Venice*

12 *Crazy* about a dance popular
in the 1960s
additive
ROUND THE TWIST –
round + the twist

14 *Hairstyle popular in Utah?*
cryptic definition
BEEHIVE (nickname for
Utah)

16 *Severe* south wind close to
coastline
additive
AUSTERE – Auster (a proper
noun) + E

17 A rugby player, very large *by
the way*
additive
A PROPOS – a prop + OS

19 *Hors d'oeuvre* with portion of
bread, and sponge to follow
additive

ROLLMOP – roll + mop

21 *Comedian* in lace factory I
scold constantly? <u>On the
contrary</u>
additive incl. reversal
SPIKE MILLIGAN – spike +
mill + I to reversed nag

24 *Female figure* in Rabat in
<u>assassination</u>
anagram
BRITANNIA – in Rabat in*

25 *Pole* maiden has to carry at
the front
additive
TOTEM – tote + M

26 *Soccer team* finding *time for a
drink?*
double definition
ELEVEN

27 *Drum* major's beginning <u>to
get in</u> my punt – a <u>lunatic</u>
sandwich incl. anagram
TYMPANUM – m inside my
punt a*

Down

1 Murdoch's to produce *a comic strip?*
additive
RUPERT BEAR – Rupert + bear

2 The Parisian one certainly
provides *relaxation*
additive
LEISURE – le + I sure

3 Quietly go ahead and *claim*
additive
PLEAD – p + lead

4 *Country* line, the nicest <u>possibly</u>
anagram

LIECHTENSTEIN – line the nicest*

6 Ring <u>about</u> society girl's *notice*
sandwich
DISMISSAL – S + miss inside dial

7 <u>Sounds like</u> a catch for *a girl*
homophone
ANNETTE – a net

8 *A legal document,* <u>whichever way you look at it</u>
reversal (palindrome)
DEED

11 *Remarkable* run on old bicycle
additive
EXTRAORDINARY – extra + ordinary

13 Holding on to old lady *not saying a word*
additive

KEEPING MUM – keeping + Mum

15 Elected soldier *behind closed doors*
additive
IN PRIVATE – in + private

18 *Rest* of English giving support to <u>turbulent</u> priest
anagram
RESPITE – priest* + E

20 *Unit of explosive power* – got name <u>wrong</u>
anagram
MEGATON – got name*

22 *18?* Could get grant at university
additive
LET UP – let + up (definition: respite from 18 down)

23 *All there* <u>over in</u> Kinm**el bay**
hidden reversal
ABLE

Puzzle 4: Sunday Times

Across

1 Leave to the end tab that's for *an American singer*
additive
BILLIE HOLIDAY – bill + ie + holiday = leave

8 Seamen with daughter *run for it*
additive
ABSCOND – ABs +con + d

9 No smooth <u>backing</u> in *structure on bottom of ship*
reversal
KEELSON – reversed no sleek

11 *Notable Mousetrap attraction*
double definition
BIG CHEESE (notable noun)

12 *Eastern inn* <u>used by</u> les**ser air**line
hidden
SERAI

13 *Rogue* to be announced <u>in</u> tabloid
sandwich
RATBAG – tba inside rag

14 Indeed *so* <u>flipping</u> *unfair*
anagram
ONE-SIDED – indeed so*

17 *They could be* <u>shifting</u> *in the chase*

all-in-one anagram
CHEETAHS – the chase*

19 *Composition*'s very good with a beat <u>returning</u>
additive incl. reversal
SONATA – so + reversed a tan

22 *Slightly wet* Chinese communist article <u>discounted</u>
takeaway
MOIST – M(a)oist

24 *Forty-five* <u>right for second tenor</u> in Italian musical foursome
letter switch
QUARTER TO – quartetto with r for t

25 A <u>cracking</u> lodge in *US city*
sandwich
SEATTLE – a inside settle

26 One <u>terribly boring</u> fat *man*
sandwich incl. anagram
LEONARD – one* inside lard

27 <u>Reformatory</u> *man to charm head of state, ER*
all-in-one additive incl. anagram
THOMAS CRANMER – man to charm S* + ER (Edward Rex)

Down

2 *Clear understanding* in place <u>for auditors</u>
additive incl. homophone
INSIGHT – in + sight (site)

3 Latrine hard <u>work</u>? Nothing <u>in</u> it with *say, Ajax*
sandwich incl. anagram
LIONHEART – O inside latrine H*

4 <u>Gutted</u> England side <u>un-</u>expectedly *goes down the plughole*
additive incl. anagram
EDDIES – E(nglan)d + side*

5 Forsaken <u>wild</u> *plants*
anagram
OAK FERNS – forsaken*

6 *Thoughts* of top team as <u>getting relegated</u>
letter switch
IDEAS – A side with as lowered

7 Charlie got better opener <u>out</u> *without doubt*
additive incl. takeaway
ASSURED – ass + (c)ured

8 <u>Absurd</u> but clear aims I <u>put out</u> as a *writer*
anagram incl. takeaway
ALBERT CAMUS – but clear a(i)ms* (absurdist movement)

10 Nothing <u>inspires</u> English rock *singer*
additive incl. sandwich
NEIL DIAMOND – E inside nil + diamond

15 *Defeat* appeared <u>to restrict</u> Old Testament study
sandwich
SHOOT DOWN – OT do inside shown

16 *Major retreat in the past, for example* in *board game*
double definition
CHEQUERS (former PM John Major)

18 *Commemoration*: mine's <u>in messy</u> heap
sandwich incl. anagram
EPITAPH – pit inside heap*

20 *Start of crop area, for example*

could be represented as this
all-in-one anagram
ACREAGE – c area eg*

21 Standard <u>clothing</u> lines on order primarily showing *little colour*

sandwich
PALLOR – ll o in par

23 *Sort of pole* to carry with difficulty on motorway
additive
TOTEM – tote + M

Puzzle 5: The Oldie

Across

1 *Pickets* prevent <u>turning</u>
reversal
POSTS – reversed stop

4 *Brutal* jibe, <u>terribly</u> sour
additive incl. anagram
BARBAROUS – barb + sour*

9 *Least* sharp point by saint
additive
TINIEST – tine + St

10 Greeting <u>in</u> moment <u>brought about</u> with English *language*
additive incl. sandwich and reversal
CHINESE – hi in reversed sec + E

11 One speaks furiously <u>about</u> leading pair of riotous *pests*
sandwich
IRRITANTS – ri inside I rants

12 Want <u>endlessly</u> to meet resistance? *Certainly not*
additive incl. takeaway
NEVER – nee(d) + R

14 HEART (central letters of wordplay in across clues omitted): **all across central letters spell SAINT VALENTINE'S DAY**

16 *Tooth* hurt, broken by ring
sandwich
MOLAR – O in mar

18 *Blushing* doctor <u>rejected</u>
reversal
RED – reversed Dr

19 *Objective editor*
double definition
END

20 *Valued* expensive <u>round</u>
reversal
RATED – reversed dear

21 *Depict* quiet worker, for instance
additive
PAINT – p + ant

23 <u>Unusual</u> gear *selection*
anagram
RANGE – gear*

25 *Frustrating* pressure group led by bad actor
additive
HAMPERING – ham + P + ring

28 Inactive, right away, with energy *cut*
additive incl. takeaway
TOPSIDE – to(r)pid + E

30 *Cause of rust* on taxi <u>in bad condition</u>
anagram
OXIDANT – on taxi*

31 Hours one <u>put into</u> musical

process releasing emotions
sandwich
CATHARSIS – hrs I inside
Cats

32 *Composer* possessed by ultimate in inspiration
additive
HAYDN – had + n

Down

1 *Querulous* in the pits, <u>troubled</u>
anagram
PETTISH – the pits*

2 Rocket <u>containing</u> new *echo-sounding equipment*
sandwich
SONAR – n inside soar

3 *Onlooker* cops treat <u>roughly</u>
anagram
SPECTATOR – cops treat*

4 Embargo, <u>inhibiting</u> to *staff*
sandwich
BATON – to inside ban

5 Crooks worked with top *firm*
additive incl. anagram
ROCK-SOLID – crooks* + lid

6 An <u>enthralling</u> story, *unfamiliar*
sandwich
ALIEN – lie inside an

7 *Number* **in** acti**on e**ndlessly
hidden
ONE

8 *Guided* horse round about
sandwich
STEERED – re inside steed

13 *Composer* from Germany <u>seized by</u> anger with volume <u>rising</u>
sandwich incl. reversal

VERDI – D inside reversed (ire + v)

15 *Poet* due <u>to be reviewed in</u> article
sandwich incl. anagram
AUDEN – due* inside an

16 *Incomparable* friend <u>hugging</u> companion left on ship
additive incl. sandwich
MATCHLESS – CH L inside mate + SS

17 Assistant, <u>upset about</u> error, <u>turned up</u> *to stock up*
sandwich incl. reversal
REPLENISH – reversed sin inside reversed helper

19 Despicable person, in charge after hesitation, *not consistent*
additive
ERRATIC – er + rat i/c

22 Get hint, <u>ordered</u> *to relax?* *On the contrary*
anagram
TIGHTEN – get hint*

24 *Plant* in island <u>filling</u> area <u>up</u>
sandwich incl. reversal
ERICA – I inside reversed acre

26 *Satellites* low over north and south
additive
MOONS – moo + N + S

27 One on river <u>going round</u> large *country*
sandwich
ITALY – L inside I Tay

29 Point <u>about</u> upper-class *place*
sandwich
PUT – U inside pt

Puzzle 6: Independent on Sunday

Across

1 Female left with desire for *a bit of bacon*
additive
FLITCH – add f + l + itch

4 *Instrument* in middle of craft about to <u>plunge into</u> planet
sandwich
MARACAS – (cr)a(ft) ca inside Mars

9 *One of the old people*, Bill, <u>about to enter</u> pub
sandwich incl. reversal
INCAN – reversed A/C inside inn

10 <u>Sorting out</u> e.g. crime scenes, very *quick responders handling crisis*
anagram
EMERGENCY SERVICES – eg crime scenes very*

12 *Guard* left work <u>having gone round</u> diamonds
additive incl. reversal
POLICE – reversed L op + ice

13 Cabman with fuel <u>running out</u> <u>not beginning</u> to flap in *vehicle*
anagram incl. takeaway
AMBULANCE – cabman (f)uel*

16 Bits <u>from</u> th**e rif**le put back in *sack*
hidden reversal
FIRE

19 *Haul* body of guards <u>back</u>
reversal
DRAW – reversed ward

20 *Critical times* – power to kill <u>must be curtailed</u>

takeaway
DEADLINES – deadliness less s

22 It's *distinctly possible* to enjoy extremes of lunacy
additive
LIKELY – like + l(unac)y

23 *Material* put forward for wild animal <u>to eat</u>
sandwich
APPOSITE – posit inside ape

26 *Drink*, grade A one, <u>smashing</u>!
anagram
ORANGEADE – grade A one*

27 The last word – delete or *change*?
additive
AMEND – amen + d

28 Hostile characters <u>chucked</u> *bits of stone*
anagram
EOLITHS – hostile*

29 Lord <u>going across</u> the street with *hound*
sandwich
PESTER – St inside peer

Down

1 Get lost <u>in</u> South Africa, in China, in *part of Netherlands*
sandwich
FRIESLAND – l inside SA inside friend

2 *Suffer* at home with awful dog
additive
INCUR – in cur

3 Hypocrisy associated with

one beginning to lecture <u>in</u> church – *a feature of some services*
additive incl. sandwich
CANTICLE – cant + i + L in CE

4 This person and space monster *get together*
additive
MEET – me + ET (the film)

5 *Neighbourhood* with <u>awful</u> ogre in
anagram
REGION – ogre in*

6 *State* opposing issue of publication (<u>not</u> English)
additive incl. takeaway
CONDITION – con + (e)dition

7 *Type* of na**sty Le**ftie
hidden
STYLE

8 Act <u>in</u> which name sadly gets *discredited*
sandwich incl. anagram
DEMEANED – name* inside deed

14 *What's on snooker table* in *bar*
double definition
BLACKBALL

15 *Models* no longer rather bulky – small!
additive
EXAMPLES – ex + ample + S

17 *City resident* beginning to enthuse when getting offer
additive
EAST-ENDER – e + as + tender

18 Local <u>revamped</u> before <u>alteration</u> in tea *place*
double anagram
ALLOCATE – local* + tea*

21 Struggle <u>to hold</u> line in *journey*
sandwich
FLIGHT – l = line in fight

22 Toilet with seat <u>not half</u> *wobbly*
additive incl. takeaway
LOOSE – loo + se(at)

24 *Clumsy* in gym <u>having</u> little <u>inner</u> energy
sandwich
INEPT – e inside in PT

25 Welshman's *soapbox*?
additive
DAIS – Dai + 's

....

Puzzle 7: Guardian
The theme to this puzzle was *The Sound of Music* (doh-re-mi-fa song).

Across

1 A *name* I call myself? <u>Not quite</u> – and wrong gender
takeaway
BRENDA – Brenda(n) name of setter (mi)

5 *Violent commotions* from English politician <u>in</u> international events
sandwich
TEMPESTS – E MP inside tests

9 *Where snooker players com-*

pete for *title, dramatically*
double definition
CRUCIBLE (Sheffield venue and Miller play)

10 *A party in suits, often,* in *Canadian city*
double definition
REGINA

11 *Stops selling* record, not in use <u>after remix</u>
additive incl. anagram
DISCONTINUES – disc + not in use*

13 For *summer, a drop of golden sun?*
double definition
BEAM (a summer is a large beam) (re)

14 <u>Sadly</u>, inn's gone for *modern way to announce its presence*
anagram
NEON SIGN – inns gone*

17 <u>Wretched</u> state of learner observed in *strained voice*
anagram
FALSETTO – state of L*

18 *Island* <u>going back</u> and <u>forth</u> in par**anoi**a, irr**ationa**lly
hidden and hidden reversal
IONA

20 *Kind of film* that gets roman- tic chap <u>excited</u>
anagram
PANCHROMATIC – roman- tic chap*

23 <u>In</u> some case**s I'm ple**ading *innocent*
hidden
SIMPLE

24 Run racket <u>in parts</u> of Asia, or *part of Italy*
sandwich incl. anagram

SARDINIA – r din inside Asia*

25 *Nit-picking* editor opposed to <u>cutting</u> inoffensive use of language
sandwich
PEDANTIC – (Ed + anti) inside PC (language)

26 Old man <u>guarding</u> a venerat- ed object in *temple*
sandwich
PAGODA – a god inside pa

Down

2 *With low level of concentra- tion,* so *not well done*
double definition
RARE

3 *Pharisee* at home <u>raised</u> fish and birds
additive incl. reversal
NICODEMUS – reversed in + cod + emus

4 *Religious leader* wedding Jack and Elizabeth
additive
ABBESS – AB + Bess

5 *Movie,* the scale of which is apparent in other clues
novelty
THE SOUND OF MUSIC (doh-re-mi-fa song)

6 Revolutionary <u>taking over</u> horse – *a long, long way to run*
sandwich
MARATHON – H inside Marat on (taking) (fa)

7 Note to follow so, for *work*
additive
ERGON – ergo + n (la)

8 *Thomas is example of one that*

needs no tender attachment
cryptic definition
TANK ENGINE

12 A privateer <u>at sea</u>, *righting wrongs*
anagram
REPARATIVE – a privateer*

15 Inform <u>about</u> one of the little people *using a needle pulling thread*
sandwich
STITCHING – titch inside sing (so)

16 *Extremely tough* way Irish writer leads or Hemingway

follows
additive
STERNEST – Sterne + St or St + Ernest

19 *Incite* prison in revolt
additive
STIR UP – stir + up

21 After competition each year, *a drink with jam and bread*
additive
CUPPA – cup + pa (te)

22 <u>From</u> wit**hin d**eer, *a female deer*
hidden
HIND (doh)

Puzzle 8: The Times

Across

1 Saint knowing *formality*
additive
STARCH – St + arch

4 *Spoilt* loyal spouse would acknowledge this
novelty
IMPAIRED – I'm paired

10 *Hound* doctor <u>beset by poor</u> counsel
sandwich incl. anagram
SCOUNDREL – Dr inside counsel*

11 *Not suitable* if in Paris you'll <u>return netting</u> sure-fire winner
sandwich incl. reversal
UNAPT – nap inside reversed tu

12 *Pots* we hear aren't <u>thrown</u>
anagram
EARTHENWARE – we hear aren't*

13 <u>Disregard</u> the odds in arguing for *career*
takeaway
RUN – even letters of arguing

14 *To drag one's feet* <u>around</u> British Library is a pity
sandwich
SHAMBLE – BL inside shame

17 *Dressed* dip with <u>mostly</u> mushroom <u>as filling</u>
sandwich incl. takeaway
DECENT – ce(p) inside dent

19 *Bob, for one*, locks study
additive
HAIRDO – hair + do

21 It's *fine* to stick <u>around</u> lake
sandwich
CLEMENT – L inside cement

23 *Sole* parent departs
additive

PAD - pa + d

24 Rat pack <u>mixing with</u> a hip
bureaucrat
anagram
APPARATCHIK - rat pack a
hip*

26 A local office <u>dispensing
with</u> its leader for *stock holding?*
takeaway
RANCH - (b)ranch

27 *Case* of drink following a
mixed dish
additive
PORTFOLIO - port + f + olio

29 Such *bowling* hypnotized
member
additive
UNDERARM - under + arm

30 *Master* to bring into play
<u>outside</u> pawn
sandwich
EXPERT - P inside exert

Down

1 County mostly welcomes
pound with *anxiety*
sandwich incl. takeaway
SUSPENSE - pen inside
Susse(x)

2 *Fling* protection if initial
resistance <u>disappears</u>
takeaway
AMOUR - a(r) mour

3 *Fleece* is being worn under
coat at first
additive
CON - C + on

5 *Duck* fat mother's left on top
additive
MALLARD - ma + L + lard

6 *What André has* is a sweet
way of speaking
additive
ACUTE ACCENT - a + cute
+ accent

7 *Tidy up* behind the cooker
additive
REARRANGE - rear + range

8 *Seeing* lawman can start to
grate
additive
DATING - DA + tin + g

9 Iron <u>round</u> girdle's *tasselled
edge*
sandwich
FRINGE - ring inside Fe

13 *Retailer* had her bears
<u>repaired</u>
anagram
HABERDASHER - had her
bears*

16 *Wild* opening group's <u>in</u>
trailer
sandwich
ABANDONED - band one
inside ad

18 Porter <u>boxing</u> fish, <u>not</u> hard
to watch closely
sandwich incl. takeaway
STAKE OUT - (h)ake inside
stout

20 *Theoretically* propane
<u>explodes</u>
anagram
ON PAPER - propane*

21 <u>When</u> time <u>is</u> right serviceman gets *poison*
letter switch
CURARE - r replacing t in
curate

22 Copy Roman Catholic university's *outline*
additive

APERÇU – ape + RC + U

25 <u>Some</u> Apocryp**hal ve**rses *cut
by fifty percent*
hidden

HALVE

28 *Trick one with brush*
double definition
FOX

....

Puzzle 9: The Week

Across

1 *Rearrange* equipment <u>re-
stricting</u> English judge
sandwich
REJIG – E J inside rig

4 A pet shoot <u>organised</u> in
back number
anagram
OSTEOPATH – a pet shoot*

9 Rascal <u>in</u> suit *falls*
sandwich
CASCADE – cad inside case

10 *One denies* bit of trouble with
Orange <u>mobile</u>
anagram
NEGATOR – t Orange*

11 Men's underwear from New
York <u>not right</u> for *photos*
takeaway
SHOTS – sho(r)ts

12 Long time <u>taken in</u> Perth
<u>working</u> on English *tabloid
feature*
**additive incl. sandwich
and anagram**
PAGE THREE – age inside
Perth* + E

14 *Brass-making work that's of
little merit?*
cryptic definition
POTBOILER – brass = money

16 *Volunteers a letter from Greece*
double definition
THETA (The TA)

17 Keep <u>bottles</u> of *white wine*
sandwich
SOAVE – o = of inside save

19 Tweet <u>heard</u> by sailor is
second-rate
additive incl. homophone
CHEAPJACK – sounds like
cheep + jack

21 Opened <u>engaging</u> film <u>al-
most</u> *without distribution*
sandwich incl. takeaway
UNDIVIDED – vide(o) inside
undid

24 Look <u>around</u> outskirts of
Rimini for *a top spot*
sandwich
EYRIE – R(imin)i inside eye

26 Plunging neckline <u>in</u> a
bolero, say leads to *amorous
approach*
sandwich
ADVANCE – V inside a dance

28 Detective's <u>keeping</u> broadcast *rejects*
sandwich
DISOWNS – sown inside DIs

29 *Gate* in <u>ground</u> lets in Rugby
Union team initially
anagram
TURNSTILE – lets in RU t*

30 Name <u>for</u> 500 stylish men,
people barely seen
letter switch

NUDES – N for D in dudes.
THE PENNY is formed from
initials letters dropped.

Down

1 *Follows* run *in* stitches
sandwich
(T)RACKS – r inside tacks

2 Nice sauce taken by all there
recently released
additive
JUST OUT – jus + tout (gravy
and all in Nice)

3 *Former PM* left <u>to inspire</u>
young man on street
sandwich
GLADSTONE – lad St inside
gone = left

4 *Having an advantage,* new
German <u>goes into</u> work
sandwich
ONE-UP – neu inside op

5 *College* board <u>no</u> good
takeaway
(E)TON – (g)et on

6 *Nothing* new <u>for</u> doctor in
water shortage
letter switch
(N)OUGHT – n for Dr in
drought

7 High tea <u>includes</u> celebrity, *a
goddess*
sandwich incl. anagram
ASTARTE – star inside tea*

8 *One's high on punch* but journalist <u>keeps</u> sober <u>surpris-
ingly</u>
sandwich incl. anagram
HORSEBACK – sober* inside
hack

13 *Eat a lot* of *Cheddar?*
double definition
GORGE

14 *Candidate* put on last <u>broad-
cast</u>
anagram
POSTULANT – put on last*

15 *Put down* in French square
close to boulevard
additive
(P)LACED – place +
(boulevar)d

16 What many Ascot gentlemen
have for *somebody*
additive
TOP PERSON – toppers on

18 Hampshire town supporting
hospital *transfer*
additive
(H)ANDOVER – H + Andover

20 <u>Harry</u> or Andrew *contracted*
anagram
(N)ARROWED – or Andrew*

22 Uniform leads to terribly
stuffy *competitions*
additive
(E)VENTS – even + t(erribly)
s(tuffy)

23 *Avoid a large American car*
double definition
DODGE

25 *Baker's supply* indeed <u>con-
taining</u> a stone
sandwich
(Y)EASTS – a st inside yes

27 *Biblical high priest*'s story:
<u>the last shall be first</u>
letter switch
ELI – lie with e moved to
first position

Puzzle 10: The i newspaper

Across

1 <u>Recalled</u> a celebration mass in *Spanish port*
   reversal
   MALAGA – reversed a gala m

4 *Urgent job once grapes are picked?*
   double definition
   PRESSING

9 Smoke rings *forbidden*
   additive
   TABOO – tab = smoke + OO = rings

10 <u>In</u> most of island people accepted *wage rise*
   sandwich incl. takeaway
   INCREMENT – men inside in Cret(e)

11 In Natal get <u>lost</u>, *deviating from course*
   anagram
   TANGENTIAL – in Natal get*

12 *Test* <u>shortened</u> *for a* **l**earner
   hidden
   ORAL

14 Obtain most offensive German article <u>about</u> radical *writer*
   sandwich
   GERTRUDE STEIN – r inside get rudest ein

16 <u>Various</u> irons too light for *one interested in birdies?*
   anagram
   ORNITHOLOGIST – irons too light*

18 *Duck* leaves lake
   additive
   TEAL – tea + l

19 Member of Oasis taking part <u>in</u> pop *congress?*
   sandwich
   PARLIAMENT – Liam inside parent

22 *I'll treat lawn*, one with nasty mark left by <u>wild</u> fire
   additive incl. anagram
   SCARIFIER – scar + i + fire*

23 African dictator introducing order, in *a manner of speaking*
   additive
   IDIOM – Idi (Amin) + OM = order

24 A river <u>goes through</u> city, *one in Scotland*
   additive incl. sandwich
   ABERDEEN – A + Dee inside Bern

25 *Animated character full of cold*
   cryptic definition
   SNEEZY – Disney character

Down

1 New York opera's <u>suppressing</u> old time *pieces of music*
   sandwich
   MOTETS – o t inside Met's

2 Country <u>exiling</u> an *80s singer*
   takeaway
   LE BON – Leb(an)on

3 *Travels* to Brest as <u>arranged</u> following journey <u>across</u> Channel at last
   additive incl. sandwich and anagram
   GLOBETROTS – l (from Channel) inside go = journey + to Brest*

5 *Two causes of disaster in the main* for *a musician*
double definition
ROCK AND ROLLER – rock & roller

6 *Twist a lot*
double definition
SLEW

7 I get close to home *showing determination*
additive
IN EARNEST – I + near nest

8 *Enjoy friendly relations? Piffle*
double definition
GET ALONG

10 *Maybe how* I've got trainer <u>repaired</u>
anagram
INTERROGATIVE – I've got trainer*

13 *Guess* I'm <u>stuck in</u> English Channel **sandwich**
ESTIMATION – I'm inside E station = channel

14 Soldier meets new friend at top *watering hole*
additive
GIN PALACE – GI + n + pal + ace

15 *Noble* precursor of Labour's ISA
additive
CONTESSA – con + Tessa

17 *Short, thickset* and fox-y?
additive
STUMPY – stump = fox + y

20 *Frenchman* <u>turned</u> green before end of voyage
additive incl. reversal
EMILE – reversed lime + e

21 *Rear female animal*
double definition
HIND

Puzzle 11: Oxford Times

Across

1 *There'll be times when you do this*
cryptic definition
MULTIPLY

5 *Still* causing *interference*
double definition
STATIC

10 *A relative* who owns a porn shop, <u>so to speak</u>
homophone
UNCLE (pawn shop)

11 *Cut off* – not dat limb, though
novelty
DISMEMBER

12 <u>Poor</u> Dad is in *a contemptuous mood*
anagram
DISDAIN – Dad is in*

13 *You need* <u>to rake</u> *last of leaf-age piling up from this*
all-in-one anagram
OAK TREE – to rake (leafag)e*

14 *Picked up by devil?* <u>Not an accurate</u> *shot, mind!*
anagram
HINDMOST – shot mind*

16 *A bowler who may get a duck?*
double definition
DRAKE (Sir Francis)

19 <u>In</u> comb**at? Hos**tile *swordsman*
hidden
ATHOS

21 *What a pension will surely
give you in retirement*
cryptic definition
BEDSTEAD

24 *A name with micro <u>waves</u>?*
all-in-one anagram
MARCONI – a n micro*

26 Tea before noon gives you
wind
additive
TYPHOON – Typhoo n

27 Losing cat <u>can make</u> one *so
sentimental*
anagram
NOSTALGIC – losing cat*

28 *Arch* beggar's plea?
novelty
OGIVE – O give!

29 *Lion always follows this sign*
cryptic definition
CANCER

30 *Gave evidence* when a terrorist leader gets tried
additive
ATTESTED – a t(errorist)
tested

Down

1 *Like my old last bit of gateau,
<u>possibly</u>*
all-in-one anagram
MOULDY – my old (gatea)u*

2 *One who has a key role to play*
cryptic definition
LOCKSMITH

3 *Place that's white* and clean,
I'd suspect
anagram

ICELAND – clean I'd*

4 *Left with a burden? <u>Not half</u>!*
**all-in-one additive incl.
takeaway**
LADEN – l + a (bur)den*

6 *Walked* with <u>half</u> tremor, on
<u>tossing</u> deck
**additive incl. takeaway
and anagram**
TRECKED – tre(mor) + deck*
(NB. an obsolete form of
trekked)

7 *Underground bit of rhizome*
all-in-one additive
TUBER – Tube + r

8 *Armour* for CO, right?
<u>Tempered</u> steel
additive incl. anagram
CORSELET – CO r + steel*

9 <u>Theatrical</u> star does *like
chocolates*
anagram
ASSORTED – star does*

15 *This – or Cam-ford, perhaps?*
novelty
OXBRIDGE

17 *It's a man to <u>cut up</u>*
all-in-one anagram
ANATOMIST – it's a man to*

18 Phil makes this orchestra
melodious
novelty
HARMONIC – (Phil)harmonic

20 *Space for so much furniture
<u>could be</u>* so great
anagram
STORAGE – so great*

22 Work <u>in</u> hotel <u>abroad</u> is *A1*
sandwich incl. anagram
TOP-HOLE – op in hotel*

23 *Really <u>venomous</u>* denied
anagram

INDEED – denied*
25 If matted, rinse in *turps*
anagram
RESIN – rinse*

26 You'll find us leaving historian *speechless*
takeaway
TACIT – Tacit(us)

Puzzle 12: Daily Telegraph

Across

1 *Presumably it can't be played by an orchestra in front of the stage?*
cryptic definition
BACKGROUND MUSIC

9 Tom's representative inside has *some cheese*
sandwich
CAMEMBERT – member inside cat

10 *Plate of fish*
cryptic definition
SCALE

11 *Made possible* being compe-tent in the finish
sandwich
ENABLED – able inside end

12 Talk of nothing, say, but *a large French country-house*
additive incl. homophone
CHATEAU – chat + eau (sounds like O = nothing)

13 *Utilise* sheep, we hear
homophone
USE – sounds like ewes

14 How policemen operate in great numbers
double definition
IN FORCE

17 *One making many a cut on the farm*
cryptic definition
SHEARER

19 Left in Connecticut with American *medicine*
additive
LINCTUS – L + in + Ct + US

22 *Given a turn by a driver?*
cryptic definition
SCREWED

24 *Part of the theatre* that is *mine*
double definition
PIT

25 *Try to cope* with small weight of fruit
additive
GRAPPLE – gr = gram + apple

26 *Cheese* lady had going round the small house
sandwich
RICOTTA – cot inside Rita

28 *Most upset it had been split*
double definition
CUT-UP

29 Curiously I can't tire although it is *very compli-cated*
anagram
INTRICATE – I can't tire*

30 *Beastly swimmer that might be found in Scotland?*
cryptic definition
LOCH NESS MONSTER

Down

1 <u>New</u> biological trace, *it's
concerned with science of
microscopic organisms*
anagram
BACTERIOLOGICAL –
biological trace*

2 *Short break during the sentence*
cryptic definition
COMMA

3 *Better* find a good walker
additive
GAMBLER – g + ambler

4 *Late* on payment
additive
OVERDUE – over = on + due

5 *Reviews* <u>new</u> section
anagram
NOTICES – section*

6 Mother's wise having *this
treatment*
additive
MASSAGE – ma's + sage

7 *Not a leader of fashion in the
field*
cryptic definition
SCARECROW

8 *Ups and downs of a professional chess player?*
cryptic
CHEQUERED CAREER

15 *Extravagantly fanciful* <u>sort of</u>
fast antic
anagram
FANTASTIC – fast antic*

16 <u>Said</u> gang found at *a French
vineyard*
homophone
CRU – sounds like crew

18 *An involuntary contraction*
<u>from</u> a **chic**ken
hidden
HIC

20 <u>Almost</u> stopping <u>absurd</u>
movement of cricket ball
anagram incl. takeaway
TOPSPIN – stoppin(g)*

21 Old Bob needs <u>other</u> pieces
to make *a group*
additive incl. anagram
SPECIES – s + pieces*

22 Rat must <u>emerge</u> from *the
rock layer*
anagram
STRATUM – rat must*

23 Courtin' <u>disaster</u> leading to
uproar
anagram
RUCTION – courtin*

27 *A health-giving drink*
cryptic definition
TOAST (your health)

···

Puzzle 13: Sunday Telegraph

Across

1 *On course, performing rather
well* or *rather poorly*
double definition
BELOW PAR

9 Jack's appearing <u>in</u> operatic
part in *Lawrence's place*
sandwich
ARABIA – AB inside aria

10 Some tig**ers at z**oo *not the
real thing*

hidden
ERSATZ

11 Rip off, in a word, *someone who's reckless*
additive
TEARAWAY – tear + away

12 *For example, football* magazine's linked with Liverpool, say
additive
SPECTATOR SPORT – Spectator's + port

15 *Island with a lot of dance*
all-in-one additive incl. takeaway
BALI – bal(l) + I

17 What's repeatedly found in grizzly bear, possibly, or *other wild animal*
anagram
ZEBRA – z bear*

19 *Flamboyance* – it's not a word that can be seen in this clue
novelty
DASH (the punctuation is not a word)

20 Western crew showering after time for *strenuous exercise*
additive
WEIGHT TRAINING – W + eight + t + raining

23 *Wrongly perceived* young woman in front of crowd, speaking
additive incl. homophone
MISHEARD – sounds like miss + herd

25 *Interfere with* person who's entitled to hold key
sandwich
NOBBLE – B inside noble

27 *Scotch* is what drunken revellers try, initially
additive incl. anagram
THWART – what* + r(evellers) t(ry)

28 *Remove* two wives, with a third mistreated inside
sandwich incl. anagram
WITHDRAW – a third* inside ww

Down

1 European carried by rail coming to *Paddington, say*
sandwich
BEAR – E inside bar

2 *Pieced together picture of ancient lawgiver*
double definition
MOSAIC (of Moses)

3 *Misbehaving youngster*, intermittently aberrant
hidden
BRAT

4 Caught, unfortunately, outside one *Channel port*
additive incl. sandwich
CALAIS – c + I inside alas

5 I pardon a wrong, *harbouring unreasonable suspicions*
anagram
PARANOID – I pardon a*

6 *Politically co-operative* oil company retaining current skilled worker
additive incl. sandwich
BIPARTISAN – I inside BP + artisan

8 *Flamboyancy* Scrabble player can never produce
novelty
PIZZAZZ (only one Z tile in Scrabble sets)

13 *Kind of author* that takes gamble with flier, *originally*
additive
PLAYWRIGHT – play + Wright

14 Final notice *about* monarch's *round-the-world trip*
sandwich
ORBIT – R inside obit

16 *Islander*'s at home, <u>nursing</u> his arm that's <u>broken</u>
sandwich incl. anagram
IRISHMAN – his arm* inside in

18 *Not for touching*
double definition
AGAINST (think comma

after for)

21 *Sporting and jovial* male having aesthetic interests
additive
HEARTY – he + arty

22 *Insignificant type*'s critical comment on wine
double definition
NOBODY (no body)

24 *Blue swallow*
double definition
DOWN (swallow verb)

26 *Be first to play heavy metal? Doesn't sound like it*
double definition incl. two different pronunciations
LEAD

Puzzle 14: Daily Mail

Across

1 *Influential condition Elgar noted with pomp*
cryptic definition
CIRCUMSTANCE

8 *Edited* and *prepared for examination*
double definition
REVISED

9 *Unsold stock* to support record
additive
BACKLOG – back + log

11 Article men <u>rewrite</u> *relating to trade*
anagram
MERCANTILE – article men*

12 Young animal with one *chrysalis*
additive
PUPA – pup + a

14 *Type of swine* a danger <u>running around</u> middle of pen
sandwich incl. anagram
GADARENE – (p)e(n) inside a danger*

16 *Old Spanish change* put <u>into</u> plant
sandwich
PESETA – set inside pea

17 Grant's <u>regular</u> *gun*
hidden
GAT – **G**r**a**n**t**

19 *Show off* Florida relative
additive
FLAUNT – Fl + aunt

21 *Confine* remainder at court, <u>keeping</u> Irish <u>back</u>
sandwich incl. reversal
RESTRICT – Ir reversed

inside rest Ct

24 *Source of energy* at home when he <u>quits</u>
additive incl. takeaway
ATOM – at + (h)om(e)

25 Speak once (<u>badly</u>) <u>about</u> good *old birthday treat*
sandwich incl. anagram
SPONGE CAKE – g inside speak once*

27 Mark <u>grabs</u> money, a *lasting power*
additive incl. sandwich
STAMINA – m inside stain + a

28 *Knot* <u>resolved</u> in daring <u>cut with</u> middle of sword
sandwich incl. anagram
GORDIAN – (sw)o(rd) inside daring*

29 *US docker* <u>rearranged</u> organs on helm
anagram
LONGSHOREMAN – organs on helm*

Down

1 Vicar <u>turns up in</u> mixed school *with hat on*
sandwich incl. reversal
COVERED – reversed rev inside coed

2 *Rarest tuna* <u>cooked</u> here?
all-in-one anagram
RESTAURANT – rarest tuna*

3 It's more expensive going out *modernising*
additive
UPDATING – up + dating

4 Bust <u>smashed</u> by the Parisian's *hard to detect*

additive incl. anagram
SUBTLE – bust* + le

5 *Expert*'s rare <u>in</u> a church
sandwich
ARCH – r in a Ch

6 *Conspire* – lines by Unionist <u>put into</u> cipher
sandwich
COLLUDE – ll U inside code

7 <u>Fancy</u> farm foie gras? *It's thick and creamy*
anagram
FROMAGE FRAIS – farm foie gras*

10 *Promising* rain-gauge's <u>working about</u> ten maybe
sandwich incl. anagram
GUARANTEEING – ten* inside rain gauge*

13 *Beat it*; English races went ahead <u>in rising</u> gloom
sandwich incl. reversal
KETTLEDRUM – E TT led inside reversed murk

15 *Essential part of cereals*, <u>crushed</u>
all-in-one anagram incl. takeaway
EAR – (ce)rea*(ls)

18 Generate <u>broadcast</u> for *someone in second decade*
anagram
TEENAGER – generate*

20 Head <u>off</u> chaos at a party *of green hue*
additive incl. takeaway
AVOCADO (adjective) – (h) avoc + a do

22 <u>I get stuck into translating</u> a Latin *language*
sandwich incl. anagram
ITALIAN – I inside a Latin*

23 *Prominently display* Spanish
   whip
   additive
   SPLASH – Sp + lash

26 *Faction*'s victory over government
   additive
   WING – win + g

Puzzle 15: Independent

Across

5 Green light around a *tree*
   sandwich
   OAK – a inside OK

7 *Cruel* conflict <u>holds</u> it back
   sandwich
   BRUTISH – reversed it inside
   brush (conflict)

9 *One of the parrots* – <u>some</u>
   tal**k ea**sily
   hidden
   KEA

10 *Joins together* <u>to repel</u> something foul
   reversal
   KNITS – reversed stink

11 *For example, origin of goose*
   all-in-one additive
   EGG – eg + g

12 *Coats of many colours?*
   cryptic definition
   PAINT

13 *Heavens above!* The monarch's <u>put outside</u>
   sandwich
   ETHER – the inside ER

15 Helps cure <u>wrong</u> in *grave
   situation*
   anagram
   SEPULCHRE – helps cure*

18 *More work – that's ideal*
   double definition
   UTOPIA (Thomas More
   work)

19 Former copper's energy *let
   off*
   additive
   EXCUSE – ex + Cu's + E

20 <u>Corrupt</u> man copied *lots of
   games*
   anagram
   COMPENDIA – man copied*

21 Left with old ship for *slow
   passage*
   additive
   LARGO – L+ Argo

23 *Servant*'s farewell takes little
   time
   additive
   VALET – vale + t

25 *This bed's mine*
   double definition
   PIT

26 *Thrash one in school*
   double definition
   WHALE

27 *Sailor* who abandons sinking
   ship? <u>Just the opposite</u>
   reversal
   TAR – reversed rat

28 *City-state*
   double definition
   NEW YORK

29 *Drink with sympathetic companion?*
   cryptic
   TEA

Down

1 Bird that is *a fledgling*
  additive
  ROOKIE – rook + ie

2 *Antipodean state that sounds like a monarchy*
  cryptic defintion
  QUEENSLAND

3 *Ruler* providing good support for the family
  additive
  KING – kin + g

4 *Piece of Englishman's residence?*
  double definition
  CASTLE

6 At length irk PM <u>badly</u>, as *member of old order*
  anagram
  KNIGHT TEMPLAR – at length irk PM*

7 Note is *to be played again*
  additive
  BIS – B (note) + is

8 Hard work put into *dance*
  additive
  HOP – h + op

9 *Medieval adventurers* <u>organised</u> in ten ranks? Right
  anagram
  KNIGHTS ERRANT – ten ranks right*

14 *Indian money* in Peru changed by European
  additive incl. anagram
  RUPEE – Peru* + E

16 Pressure on amusing person as *safeguard*
  additive
  PRECAUTION – p + re + caution (amusing person)

17 *Watering hole used by natives*
  cryptic definition
  LOCAL

20 South American rodent <u>grabs</u> it for *a hole*
  sandwich
  CAVITY – it inside cavy

22 Partners in love? No, it's *not reciprocal*
  sandwich
  ONE-WAY – EW inside O + nay (no)

24 *Preserve money*
  double definition
  TIN

25 Vessel <u>carrying</u> wine, primarily *hock*
  sandwich
  PAWN – w inside pan

26 *Pot from East* or West acceptable
  additive
  WOK – W + OK

Chess pieces as set out on the board appear at the top of the completed grid.

4. Thanks

To Richard Heald for checking the whole text at the proof stage and suggesting improvements using his extensive crossword knowledge and skills.

To Erwin Hatch for much checking of crosswords and text at the earlier stages.

To Susie Bell, whose presentational advice and skill on layout was invaluable.

To Mike Barker, Christopher Brougham and Colin Clarke for their help with specific issues.

To all the setters, named or pseudonymous, who agreed to the re-publishing of their work. They are: Dave Crossland, Colin Dexter, Colin Gumbrell, Brian Greer, Don Manley, Paul McKenna and Allan Scott.

To all the remaining, anonymous setters whose work deserves to be acknowledged publicly and one day will be.

To crossword editors, Colin Inman, Mike Hutchinson, Phil McNeil and Hugh Stephenson, whose approval to re-publishing was needed and was readily given.

To Tony Savage for his generous foreword.

To all at HarperCollins, especially Gerry Breslin who first suggested a generic book and saw it through to completion.

To my wife Pamela for advice and support, not just for this book, but in so many ways for nearly 48 years. As she once said, she keeps my show on the road.

Index

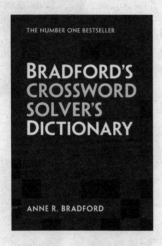
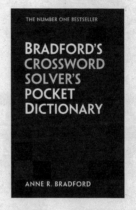
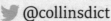

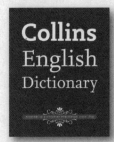
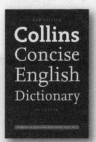
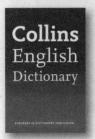
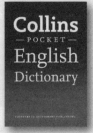
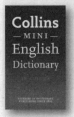

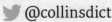